IRISH CASTLES
AND HISTORIC HOUSES

CAXTON EDITIONS
AN IMPRINT OF CAXTON PUBLISHING GROUP
20 BLOOMSBURY STREET, LONDON WC1 3QA

© CAXTON EDITIONS, 2002
© JAMES STEVENS CURL (INTRODUCTORY ESSAY)

ISBN 1 84067 417 2

A COPY OF THE CIP DATA IS AVAILABLE FROM THE
BRITISH LIBRARY UPON REQUEST

DESIGNED AND PRODUCED FOR CAXTON EDITIONS
BY POINTING DESIGN CONSULTANCY

REPROGRAPHICS BY GA GRAPHICS.

ACKNOWLEDGMENTS
THE NORTHERN IRISH TOURIST BOARD
BORD FÁILTE – THE IRISH TOURIST BOARD
TONY ROACH OF HERITAGE IMAGES
COPY EDITOR: ROSANNA NEGROTTI

IRISH CASTLES
AND HISTORIC HOUSES

EDITED BY
BRENDAN O'NEILL

WITH AN INTRODUCTORY ESSAY BY
JAMES STEVENS CURL

CAXTON EDITIONS

CONTENTS

INTRODUCTION

BY JAMES STEVENS CURL

Some early defensive fortifications survive in Ireland. They include several enclosures surrounded by dry-stone walls. Examples are Staigue Fort, Co Kerry; the Doon Fort, Naran, Co Donegal; the Grianán of Aileach, Co Donegal; and Dun Aenghus, Inis Mór, Aran. These alone are sufficient to demonstrate that Ireland has a uniquely fine collection of such structures, better than anywhere else in Europe.

Ireland possesses many castles and tower-houses, probably almost 3,000, so they are by far the most common buildings of antiquity found in the country. Most of these are actually fortified private houses, dating from the fifteenth, sixteenth, and

seventeenth centuries, and should be differentiated from castles as such, most of which were erected after the twelfth-century Anglo-Norman invasion.

Castles

Fortified towers, donjons, or keeps were among the earliest stone-built military structures. Keeps on rectangular plans (such as Carrickfergus, Co Antrim, and Adare, Co Limerick), are found, as well as those on circular plans (Dundrum, Co Down, and Inchiquin, Co Cork), and some on polygonal plans (Shanid, Co Limerick, and Dungarvan, Co Waterford). Carrickfergus Castle, though much altered over the centuries, has an inner ward, had a middle

Left: Carrickfergus Castle, Co Antrim.

ward, and has an outer ward, the whole ensemble surrounded by a wall, the plan-form of which is determined by the basalt outcrop of rock on which it is built. Two circular towers flank the entrance on the landward side, and the whole impressive ensemble dominates the harbour. Carlingford Castle, Co Louth (also called King John's Castle), has a plan-form also dictated by the rock on which it stands, and Roche Castle, also in Co Louth, was similarly constrained (as its name suggests).

Another type of castle, consisting of a rectangular building with a cylindrical tower at each corner, appeared in thirteenth-century Ireland, examples of which may be seen at Carlow, Co Carlow, and Ferns, Co Wexford. Terryglass, Co Tipperary, Enniscorthy, Co Wexford, and the original Dunluce Castle, Co Antrim, are of similar type (though the last, in its final form, had a plan dictated by the great rock upon which this MacDonnell stronghold is perched). Much larger was Quin Castle, Co Clare (within the ruins of which the later Franciscan friary was built), but although the form was the same, the area bounded by the four walls cannot have been entirely roofed over.

Later in the thirteenth century were erected several castles the design of which was related to the great Royal castles in England and Wales (such as Harlech). The Irish examples had twin-towered gate-houses (like Carrickfergus), and included Roscommon and Ballintober, both in Co Roscommon, and Ballymote, Co Sligo. They had no keeps, and in the case of Ballymote the towers were polygonal.

Other impressive castles included Askeaton, Co Limerick, with its fifteenth-century hall built above the river, and Kilkenny, Co Kilkenny (unfortunately much altered).

Right: Dunluce Castle, Co Antrim.

Tower-Houses

During the latter part of the mediaeval period there was a progressive deterioration of the Anglo-Norman feudal system and a breakdown of law and order. In the early fifteenth century, government subsidies were offered to those able to construct castles or towers in the counties of Dublin, Kildare, Louth, and Meath, but these 'ten-pound' castles were fairly basic.

More impressive was Kilclief Castle, Strangford Lough, Co Down, erected between 1412 and 1441. Projections form a recessed panel on one side, spanned at high level by an arch, a kind of giant machicolation, also found at Audley's (Strangford) and Jordan's (Ardglass) Castles, both in Co Down, and at Bunratty Castle, Co Clare, Donamon Castle, Co Roscommon, and Listowel Castle, Co Kerry.

Within tower-houses the rooms were placed one over the other, and the room on the ground floor was usually vaulted to protect the upper storeys. On occasion the vault was near the top of the tower, supporting the floor of the main chamber, and not uncommonly there were two vaults: one over the lowest floor and one supporting the top room. Irish tower-houses vary from three to six storeys high. As with many Irish ecclesiastical towers, tower-houses are battered (i.e. they taper, becoming slightly smaller with height), and they stood on a more steeply-battered plinth or *talus*, designed to cause missiles, if dropped from the top of the tower, to hit the *talus* and be deflected towards any attackers.

Some tower-houses, curiously, had no fireplaces: a hearth would have been provided in the centre of the topmost room, with a louvred opening on the roof to enable the smoke to escape. At Clara Castle, Co Kilkenny, there was an early fireplace on the second floor, with a chimney carried up in the wall. At Burnchurch Castle, Co

Kilkenny, there were fireplaces on both the second floor and uppermost level. Tower-house stairs were both circular (like at Clara Castle) and straight, though built into the walls (such as at Burnchurch). The entrance to a tower-house was usually in the middle of one of the sides (approached through a bawn, or fortified enclosure), with the stair on one side of the vestibule and a guard-room on the other. This vestibule led to the room on the ground floor, and in the ceiling of the vestibule was a 'murdering-hole' from which intruders or visitors could be inspected or, if needs be, dispatched.

Irish tower-houses often contained secret chambers in hollows within the haunches of stone vaults, as on the fourth floor of Clara Castle. A similar secret room can be seen at Carrigafoyle Castle (Ballylongford), Co Kerry. Rectangular bartizans projecting on corbels from the corners of the tower-houses enabled fire to be directed along the walls and beneath the bartizans: good examples may be found at Coolhull Castle, near Duncormick, Co Wexford, Ballynacarriga, near Dunmanway, Co Cork, and Fiddaun (or Fiddown), Co Galway. The last castle also contains an angle-loop, or a slit at the arris of the corner, with an embrasure within the wall behind: angle-loops were admirable for defence using small-arms.

None of these tower-houses stood alone as objects in the landscape (as many of them do today). They were either built within some sort of walled enclosure (such as Dungory [Dunguaire], near Kinvara [Kinvarra], Co Galway – which also had a flanker [or fortified tower] at one of the corners), or had a walled forecourt in front of the entrance (as at Clara Castle). Both enclosures were called 'bawns' (from *bábhun*, an enclosure), meaning a sort of pound for cattle. Some tower-houses had halls built against one wall of the tower. Windows were generally very small, but from the middle of the sixteenth century

became larger, with mullions and transoms (such as at Knockkelly, Co Tipperary).

So why did so many tower-houses survive in Ireland? They were never intended to resist sieges from artillery, and indeed could not have done so. The terrain in Ireland (and poor infrastructure) meant that heavy ordnance could only be moved around with enormous difficulty and expense, and so artillery was only (or mostly) used on large and significant targets, towns, or major fortresses. They could, and did, resist marauders, lawless bands, and the like, however, and so remained useful until comparatively late in historical terms, which partly explains their continuing presence in the Irish landscape.

Some (though not many) tower-houses were built on circular plans: they include Ballynahow, near Thurles, Co Tipperary, which had two of its three floors fully vaulted. One of the most curious circular tower-houses is Newtown Castle, the

Burren, Co Clare, which is essentially a cylinder atop a tall pyramid, so the effect is of four 'broaches' or 'spurs' under the cylinder. Thus the cylinder describes an elliptical curve on the steep slope of the pyramid below, and a triangular notch is cut at the base of the ellipse at the apex of which is a gun-loop enabling fire to be directed over the whole of the battered wall or *talus* below. A variant of this principle occurs at Ballynamona Castle, Co Cork, a rectangular tower at the lower parts of which are four battered triangular-topped recesses at the apices of which are gun-loops, so that fire could be similarly directed below.

Other 'castles' are larger, and include Blarney, Co Cork, a fifteenth-century building erected by the McCarthys. Its walls are very thick, but get progressively thinner with each storey, thus seatings are provided for the floors and the habitable space gets bigger with height. The castle is crowned with high crenellations supported by massive corbels.

Left: Blarney Castle, Co Cork.

Several Irish towns contained numerous tower-houses, as an Elizabethan drawing of Carrickfergus, Co Antrim, makes clear. According to that source, there were ten crenellated tower-houses in addition to terraces of single-storey houses, some detached cottages, and some seventy or more Irish 'beehive' huts, placed with no regard whatsoever for any sense of urban design. Urban tower-houses survive in Ardglass, Co Down, Carlingford, Co Louth, and Dalkey, Co Dublin. It is said that both Galway and Kilmallock (Co Limerick) once had many stone tower-houses, but not much in the way of evidence survives today.

Late-Sixteenth- and Seventeenth-Century Large Houses

The unsettled condition of Elizabethan Ireland was such that not much in the way of significant domestic architecture was erected, and what was achieved was fortified. One of the most impressive houses is Rathfarnham Castle, Co Dublin, almost square, of three storeys over a basement, with a sharply-pointed flanker at each corner. Erected in the 1590s, Rathfarnham Castle was built for Adam Loftus (c.1533-1605), who had arrived in Ireland in 1560, and rapidly rose to a position of some eminence (he was consecrated Archbishop of Armagh in 1563). Very similar in plan was Raphoe Palace, Co Donegal, dated 1636, erected for the Anglican Bishop John Leslie (1571-1671), and sharply pointed flankers recurred at Manorhamilton, Co Leitrim (c.1634). Large square corner-towers or flankers were built at several sites, including Portumna Castle, Co Galway (c.1610), and Burntcourt (Burncourt), Co Tipperary (c.1640). By then, typically English mullioned and transomed windows with hood-moulds over them had become *de rigueur*, and may be found where large extensions were made to existing tower-houses (such as at Leamaneagh [or Leamaneh] Castle, Co Clare [for an old Irish family], and at Donegal Castle, Co Donegal [for the English family of Brooke],

Rathfarnham Castle, Co Dublin.

where the Jacobean manor-house wing is very much an English seventeenth-century *house*, as opposed to a castle, even though it is within a defensive bawn and protected by the adjacent fifteenth-century O'Donnell stronghold). On occasion, gabled houses with mullioned and transomed windows have circular flankers, as at Killenure, Dundrum, Co Tipperary, home of the O'Dwyers.

After the Flight of the Earls in 1607 and the beginnings of the Ulster Plantation, several fortified manor-houses were built by the Livery Companies of the City of London, several with fortified bawns and flankers, but not many of these survive. Vestiges remain, however, at Ballykelly, Movanagher, Bellaghy, Brackfield, Moneymore, and Salterstown, Co Londonderry. Two circular flankers can be seen at Dalway's Bawn, Co Antrim, complete with mullioned windows, but this fortified English house was not connected with the Londoners in any way, because the City of London's estates were

all in Co Londonderry, a county specially created for the purpose from the County of Coleraine to which parts of Counties Antrim, Donegal, and Tyrone were added. Dalway's Bawn, however, shows how unsettled seventeenth-century Ulster was, even in the ancient Counties of Antrim and Down, where there had been a powerful Anglo-Norman presence ever since the twelfth century.

Strong Scots influences may be detected at the Watergate, Enniskillen Castle, Co Fermanagh, with its twin corbelled circular tourelles (probably *c.*1609), and also at Monea Castle (begun 1618) in the same county. The latter is essentially a rectangular tower-house (protected by the usual vaulted ground floor), with two cylindrical towers flanking one of the short sides, set on either side of the entrance. These towers have corbels at the top on which sit square cap-houses with crow-stepped gables, and it is these that give the building its overwhelmingly Scots

Left: Enniskillen Castle, Co Fermanagh.

appearance (compare Claypotts Castle, Broughty Ferry, Angus). Between the towers of Monea Castle is a high arch, similar to that at Kilclief, Co Down, mentioned above. Also indubitably Scots in their architectural treatment are Ballygally Castle, Co Antrim, with its corbelled cylindrical tourelles surmounted by conical roofs, and Killyleagh Castle, Co Down, both originally erected in the 1620s, although Killyleagh was considerably re-edified (1847-51) to designs by Charles Lanyon (1813-89), and became rather more Gallic in the process, reminiscent, perhaps, of aspects of Falkland Palace, Fife.

Instability during the seventeenth century is made clear by the erection of buildings such as Coppinger's Court, Co Cork (probably 1630s), which had massive machicolations, and a plan closely resembling Richhill Castle, Co Armagh. The latter acquired curved gables later, but its essential form points to a probable date earlier than that normally credited to it.

Space precludes a consideration of more of the 'castles' and fortified houses that can be found in many parts of Ireland, so we must move on to the period after the Battle of Aughrim (1691) which heralded a century of peace in Ireland. Although defence was still a preoccupation in late-seventeenth-century Ireland (as can be seen from the plans of Annegrove, near Carrigtohil, Co Cork, where the house had four flanker-towers, but was otherwise quite up-to-date in its arrangement), influences from the Netherlands and England began to come in, and some houses shed all references to defence. An example was an interesting house of the 1660s or 1670s called Eyrecourt, Co Galway (now virtually wholly demolished). One of the most pleasing seventeenth-century unfortified houses to survive is Springhill, Moneymore, Co Londonderry, built c.1680. It was originally surrounded by a defensive bawn. Two single-storey wings were added to the main house in c.1765, and it was also at that time when the entrance-front acquired its present arrangement of seven windows across

Springhill, Moneymore, Co Londonderry.

Interior at Russborough, Blessington, Co Wicklow.

its width. Another seventeenth-century house of *c*.1664 was enlarged and extended for his own use by the Dublin architect, George Ensor in *c*.1770: this was Ardress House, Charlemont, Co Armagh, and it contains some good plasterwork.

The Eighteenth and Nineteenth Centuries

The really glorious period for the Irish country house was the eighteenth century, beginning with the splendid Castletown, Co Kildare (*c*.1722), designed by Alessandro Galilei (1691-1737), and begun under the direction of Edward Lovett Pearce (*c*.1699-1733), who was to become one of the most important Palladian architects working in eighteenth-century Ireland. Galilei had designed the huge thirteen-window-wide three-storey-over-basement palazzo-like main block, and Pearce added the lower two-storey wings, joined to the main block by elegant colonnaded quadrants.

Sir Edward Lovett Pearce (as he became in 1732) was related to Sir John Vanburgh (1664-1726), and took as his assistant the German-born architect, Richard Cassels (or Cassel, or Castle) (*c*.1690-1751). Together they seem to have been responsible for the grand palatial house (now ruined) known as Summerhill, Co Meath, which also had wings linked to the main block by quadrants, and was more Vanbrughian than Palladian. Pearce designed Bellamont Forest, Co Cavan (*c*.1730), Ireland's first mature Palladian villa, and Cassels designed Ballyhaise, also in Co Cavan (1733), which has two important features: a stone frontispiece with superimposed Ionic and Doric pilasters; and a semi-elliptical projection or bow on the rear elevation, suggesting Continental Baroque exemplars, and indicating the elliptical saloon behind. Cassels was the architect of Russborough, Blessington, Co Wicklow (1741-50), the most mature of all Irish Palladian country houses, with exquisite Baroque and Rococo plasterwork inside. The handsome wings are joined to the central block by means of colonnaded quadrants, and on either side of the wings are walled courts, each entered through Baroque archways. Of course there are numerous smaller Georgian houses, few of them attributable to known architects, but there are others which are noble works. Among the finest Irish country houses may be mentioned Castletown Cox, Co Kilkenny (built in the 1770s, to designs by the relatively obscure Davis Ducart or Duckart [or Daviso d'Arcort – *fl. c.*1760, d. 1786]), with ashlar and internal plasterwork of superb quality. Ducart has been described as a Sardinian or Piedmontese, or a 'Savoyard', and as the 'last Palladian in Ireland'. He designed Kilshannig, Rathcormac, Co Cork (1765-6 – another fine house of Franco-Italian appearance), and may have influenced the design of the arcaded wings (*c.*1768) at Florencecourt, Co Fermanagh (*c.*1758 or *c.*1764), though the main central block is far too uncertain and gauche to have been by any great architect, and is probably the work of someone more dependent upon pattern-books and textbooks of architectural details than on any grand vision. The wings and internal Rococo plasterwork, however, are of a higher order, even though the house had to be restored after a disastrous fire in the 1950s.

Very pretty is Castle Ward, Co Down (1760s), Palladian on one side and Georgian Gothick on the other (with interiors following the same stylistic trends), but the architect is not yet known, although he may have come from the Bristol area. A possible candidate, however, could be James Bridges, who practised in Bristol between 1757 and 1763. The Ward family had strong connections with Bristol, and Bridges's work there has similarities to Castle Ward. Grey Abbey (also called Rosemount), Grey Abbey, Co Down, was built in 1762, so is almost contemporary with Castle Ward, and has similar Gothick windows on the ground storey of the canted bay on the garden front, but its Gothick work may date from 1782 or afterwards, so was inspired by Castle Ward.

Right: Castle Ward, Co Down.

Even prettier is Caledon House, Co Tyrone, begun in 1779 to designs by Thomas Cooley (*c*.1740-84), but altered and extended by John Nash (1752-1835) in 1808-10, who added the screen of coupled Ionic columns between two pavilions to the north front. Nash also designed Killymoon Castle, Cookstown, Co Tyrone (*c*.1803), a free, asymmetrical, crenellated composition with round and square towers. It has Regency Gothick interiors, and is a good example of Nash's skills as a designer of agreeably disposed houses in which complex geometries in the plan-form, combined with asymmetry, create buildings that are both pretty and amusing.

Caledon's south front has a projecting half-elliptical bow, behind which is the so-called Oval Drawing-Room. The bowed feature is again found, this time with a Giant Order of Ionic columns, at Castle Coole, Co Fermanagh, a superb house of 1790-7 designed by James Wyatt (1746-1813), with an Ionic portico, flanking Doric

Left: Castle Coole, Co Fermanagh.

colonnaded wings and enchanting interiors. The Neo-Classical tendencies present at Caledon and Castle Coole were more rigorously and severely expressed at Lissadell, Carney, Co Sligo (1830-5), designed by Francis Goodwin (1784-1835) for the Gore-Booth family. The exterior employs only *antæ* for its articulation, and the sharp Grecian geometries of the interior show Goodwin (whose practice was in the North of England) to be a much underrated architect, whose work should be more appreciated and better-known.

The Ionic Giant Order on a bow recurs at Ballyfin, Mountrath, Co Laois (or Leix), of 1821-6, designed by the father-and-son practice of Sir Richard (1767-1849) and William Vitruvius (1794-1838) Morrison: it is one of the finest nineteenth-century Neo-Classical country houses in Ireland, but the Morrisons may not have been entirely responsible for the work, as Dominic Madden (*fl.* 1820-31 – better known for his designs for the Roman Catholic Church)

was involved at the beginning. W.V. Morrison remodelled Baronscourt, Co Tyrone (*c.*1832), a house begun in 1779-82 by George Steuart (*c.*1730-1806 – a Gaelic-speaking Highland Scot, whose works in and around Shrewsbury, Shropshire, are justly celebrated), but subsequently (1780s) altered by John Soane (1753-1837). Unfortunately, the house was gutted by fire in 1796, and after that Soane's office appears to have carried out remedial works, but these were virtually obliterated by Morrison's extensive alterations and additions (especially the opulent interiors). In 1947 Sir Albert Edward Richardson (1880-1964) tidied things up, added the colonnade, and reduced the wings. In 1975 some of the interiors were reinstated as Morrison designed them. W.V. Morrison was also the architect of Glenarm Castle and 'Barbican' Gate, Glenarm, Co Antrim (1823-4 – Tudor Gothic), and of Mountstewart, Ards Peninsula, Co Down (1825-8 – Neo-Classical). Both houses have had alterations done to their interiors in the twentieth century that are not, perhaps, entirely appropriate for the architecture.

Hillsborough Castle, Hillsborough, Co Down, was largely created by Robert William Furze Brettingham (*c*.1750-1820) in *c*.1795-7 for the Downshire family, but was enlarged in the 1830s and 1840s to designs by Thomas Duff (*c*.1792-1848). Later, James Sands (*fl*. 1813-46), a pupil of James Wyatt, appears to have carried out some works there in 1844. From 1925 the Castle became known as Government House, and was the residence of successive Governors of Northern Ireland: in 1973 the post of Governor was abolished, and in 2002 the Castle is used as the official residence of Secretaries of State for the Province.

One of the loveliest of all Classical houses in Ireland was Townley Hall, Drogheda, Co Louth (begun 1793), designed by Francis Johnston (1760-1829), with its extraordinarily beautiful top-lit cantilevered stair. But, as the nineteenth century progressed, a fashion for things Gothic began to make itself felt. The gatehouse of Birr Castle, Co Offaly, became the core of what is now known as Birr Castle (which looks more like a charming Georgian Gothick confection). Some of the most enjoyable parts were created by Lawrence Parsons, 2nd Earl of Rosse (1758-1841), assisted by the architect and contractor, John Johnston, and include the saloon of 1801-2. Another example of Georgian Gothick, this time of superb quality, is Charleville Forest, Tullamore, Co Offaly, amateurish drawings for which were prepared by Charles William Bury, from 1800 Viscount, and from 1806 1st Earl of Charleville (the title is now extinct), but Francis Johnston was the architect who provided the expertise to transmogrify the designs into more professional drawings. Masterful and grand are the entrance hall and stair, and the spectacular gallery with beautiful plaster fan-vaulting.

Much grander is Adare Manor, Adare, Co Limerick, built as the seat of the Earls of Dunraven, with which A.W.N. Pugin (1812-52) was connected from 1846, followed by P.C. Hardwick (1822-92). Unfortunately, all the contents have been dispersed, but the building still may be enjoyed. William White (1825-1900) was the architect of one of the most impressive of all Irish Victorian country houses, Humewood Castle, Kiltegan, Co Wicklow, complete with Irish crenellations, crow-step gables, and machicolations, built 1867-70 for W. W. F. Dick (formerly Hume), MP.

Occasionally, the Romanesque style was used for country houses, but not often. The grandest essay in Romanesque domestic architecture in Ireland is Gosford Castle, Markethill, Co Armagh (1819-21), by Thomas Hopper (1776-1856), which, at the time of writing, faced an uncertain future. Another example of a large Irish country house in the Norman style was Glenstal Castle, Moroe, Co Limerick

(1838-9), designed by the Suffolk-born William Bardwell (1795-1890): the entrance is set between massive cylindrical towers (reminiscent of Rockingham Castle, Northamptonshire), and the main doorway in the courtyard is a copy (1841) of that at Killaloe Cathedral, Co Clare.

Other mediaevalising Irish country houses include Dromore Castle, Pallaskenry, Co Limerick (1867-73). Designed for William Hale John Charles Pery, 3rd Earl of Limerick (1840-96), by Edward William Godwin (1833-86) as a composition of exceptional quality, not only archaeologically correct, but beautifully composed and partly designed for defence (the period of building was the time of the Fenian disturbances). Reminiscent of the Rock of Cashel, its ruins are as poignantly beautiful. Godwin was also responsible for the design of Glenbeigh Towers, Glenbeigh, Co Kerry (1876-71 – burnt out 1922), a fortress-house in the form of a massive keep erected for the Hon Rowland Winn (1816-88), whose son, Rowland, 5th Baron Headley (1855-1935) converted to Islam. At the time, the landowning classes must have seen the writing on the wall, and responded with a defensive architecture that somehow reflected their plight. Both Dromore Castle and Glenbeigh Towers are eloquent testaments to the restless state of Ireland at the time, but one of the most remarkable (and little-known) Irish country houses (also burnt out in 1921) was Dunboy Castle, Castletownberehaven, West Cork, the design for an extension to which was commissioned in 1865 by the copper magnate, H.L. Puxley, from a London architect, John Thomas Christopher (*c*.1829-1910), a former pupil of Robert Garland (1808-63) who, as Surveyor to The Salters' Company, had designed the Manor House and other buildings at Magherafelt, Co Londonderry. Christopher's designs included an enormous hall spanned by stone arches that in turn carry arches supporting the clerestorey. Even as ruins they are impressive.

There were many other Irish country houses that had earlier origins, and were added to at various times. One of the noblest of all is Lismore Castle, Lismore, Co Waterford, sited on high ground above the River Blackwater. It incorporates some of the towers of the mediaeval castle of the Bishops of Lismore which itself replaced a castle erected by King John (reigned 1199-1216). In 1602 the castle was sold by Sir Walter Raleigh (*c*.1552-1618) to Richard Boyle (1566-1643), later (1620) 1st Earl of Cork, who rebuilt the castle. After various vicissitudes the building passed to the Cavendish family, and William Spencer Cavendish (1790-1858), 6th Duke of Devonshire (from 1811) re-edified it and made it inhabitable, but the work, carried out in 1811 by William Atkinson (*c*.1773-1839), involved considerable destruction. A more sensitive scheme was carried out by Joseph Paxton (1801-65) in 1850-8, who was largely responsible for the appearance of the Castle today. Pugin designed certain features of the interior.

29

Perhaps the most interesting of all old castles that has been subjected to change over the centuries is the ancestral home of the St Lawrence family at Howth Castle, Co Dublin. The oldest part is a mediaeval keep with corner-towers crowned with Irish crenellations, but there have been many additions since then, including a tower and other works, of 1910, designed by Sir Edwin Landseer Lutyens (1869-1944). The happiest parts of Lutyens's additions include the arched loggia, the entrance-hall, library, and landscaping.

Lutyens also carried out a much more comprehensive transformation of Lambay Castle, Co Dublin, from 1905, for Cecil Baring (1864-1934), later (1929) 3rd Baron Revelstoke of Membland. He made the old fort inhabitable and added much accommodation with vaulted ceilings, stone fireplaces, mullioned and transomed windows, steep pantiled roofs, gables, and

Left: Lismore Castle, Lismore, Co Waterford.

massive chimney-stacks, all composed with a great mastery of form. Lutyens also created the garden and designed (in the 1930s) the White House near the harbour for Lord Revelstoke's daughter, Daphne (1904-86), who married Arthur Joseph Lawrence Pollen in 1920.

But when we look at the remarkable legacy of Irish country houses, we cannot but be struck by the numerous fanciful compositions in various castellated styles. Was this to give the Anglo-Irish aristocracy and landowning classes a sense of belonging, or even a sense of security, for their days were clearly numbered? Among the most ambitious houses in the castle style (apart from those mentioned above) were Ashford Castle, near Cong, Co Galway (1870s), designed by James Franklin Fuller (1835-1925) and George Ashlin (1837-1921); Dromore Castle, Kenmare, Co Kerry (c.1831-38), by Sir Thomas Deane (1792-1871); the previously mentioned Dromore Castle, Pallaskenry, Co Limerick,

by Godwin; Duckett's Grove, near Carlow, Co Carlow (1830 – burnt out 1933), by Thomas A. Cobden; Gormanston Castle, Gormanston, Co Meath (early nineteenth century); Crom Castle, Newtown Butler, Co Fermanagh (1829), by Edward Blore (1787-1879); Johnstown Castle, near Wexford, Co Wexford (c.1833-6), by Daniel Robertson (fl. 1812-43 – a Scots architect, probably related to James [1732-94] and Robert [1728-92] Adam [and seemingly a contributory factor in creating the financial difficulties that beset William Adam (1738-1822) in the 1820s], who had previously designed the Oxford University Press building [1826-7] and St Clement's church, Oxford [1827-8], before leaving the City of Dreaming Spires suddenly [and under a cloud] in 1829); Jenkinstown, Ballyragget, Co Kilkenny (early nineteenth century, by William Robertson [1770-1850] of Kilkenny); Killeen Castle, Dunsany, Co Meath (altered c.1804 to designs by Francis Johnston and again in 1841 to designs by James Shiel);

Killua Castle, Clonmellon, Co Westmeath (*c*.1830), probably also by Shiel, but now a ruin; Kylemore Castle, Letterfrack, Co Galway (1860s), by J.F. Fuller; Lough Cutra Castle, Gort, Co Galway (*c*.1811 onwards), by John Nash; Markree Castle, Collooney, Co Sligo (enlarged and transformed in 1803 to designs by Francis Johnston, and again enlarged, in 1866, to designs by James Maitland Wardrop [1824-82] of Edinburgh), the entrance-gateways to the demesne of which were designed by Francis Goodwin; Narrow Water Castle, Warrenpoint, Co Down (*c*.1836), by Thomas Duff; Slane Castle, Slane, Co Meath (begun 1785 to designs by James Wyatt and completed by Francis Johnston, though other architects seem also to have been involved); and Tullynally Castle, Castlepollard, Co Westmeath (enlarged 1780 to designs by Graham Myers, Gothicised by Francis Johnston in 1801-6, enlarged again under Sir Richard Morrison in 1839-42, and further enlarged in 1860 by James Rawson Carroll [d. 1911]). There

were many more, but their castellations did not save them; they were burned in the disorder of the early 1920s, and several more fell victim to fire or neglect thereafter. Some remain as spectacular ruins (such as Wilton Castle, Enniscorthy, Co Wexford, by Robertson of Kilkenny, burnt 1923).

One of the greatest losses in recent years was the destruction by fire, in 1981, of Tynan Abbey, Co Armagh, a large castellated, gabled, pinnacled, and spired house, added to at various times, to designs possibly by, inter alia, Augustus Charles Pugin (1769-1832), James Pain (1779-1887), George Pain (1793-1838), and Nash. It was considerably extended to plans by W.J. Barre, and W.H. Lynn also prepared drawings for it in 1877. Considering that Nash was involved not far away at Caledon, parts of Tynan Abbey were very reminiscent of his work at Aqualate Hall, Forton Hall, Staffordshire (1806-10 – destroyed), so it is highly likely that Nash or his pupils, the Pains, were involved. The intruders of 1981 murdered Sir (Charles) Norman Lockhart Stronge (1894-1981), the 8th Baronet, and his son, James Matthew Stronge (1932-81). In 1988 an explosion in the cellars (probably a booby-trap) did further damage, and in 1998 the ruins of Tynan Abbey were demolished. Not surprisingly, the Stronge family (who settled in Ireland the best part of four hundred years ago) did not care to restore the house or live there again.

Apart from the Gothic, Gothick, Romanesque and Classical Georgian houses (of which there were many), Ireland can boast several Italianate houses influenced by the precedents designed by Sir Charles Barry (1795-1860): they include Ballywalter Park, Co Down, Ireland's finest Italianate palazzo, with a sumptuous interior, notably the entrance-hall and stair, erected in the 1840s to designs by Charles Lanyon; Whitfield Court, Kilmeadan, Co Waterford (*c.*1841), designed by Abraham Denny of Dublin; The Abbey, Whiteabbey, Co Antrim (*c.*1850), built by Lanyon for himself; and Dunderave, Bushmills, Co Antrim (*c.*1847-50), possibly also by Lanyon.

One of the most charming of Irish country houses is The Argory, Derrycaw, Charlemont, Co Armagh, designed in the 1820s by the somewhat obscure John and Arthur Williamson of Dublin (*fl.* 1815-37). It has Greek Doric columns flanking the entrance-porch, and the staircase is especially handsome. However, Lissadell, Carney, Co Sligo, mentioned above, remains the grandest and most severe Greek Revival house in Ireland. As far as other Revivals were concerned, there is a very curious Egyptianising entrance at Dunore House, Aldergrove, Co Antrim (1870), featuring two bucolic pharaohs, two Nubians (possibly female), all four with the Nemes head-dress, and set on blocks inscribed with hieroglyphs. The architect is unknown.

The exotic in architecture is rare in Ireland, although there are some strange

Right: The Argory, Derrycaw, Charlemont, Co Armagh.

Egyptianising and Oriental mausolea here and there. At Dromana, Cappoquin, Co Waterford, is a fine house set above the River Blackwater, and at the northern end of the demesne is an extraordinary Hindoo-Gothick gateway flanked by lodges, complete with onion-dome and very slight minaret-like finials. It is supposed to date from the 1820s, and is as charmingly unserious as Brighton Pavilion: it is the only example of this style in Ireland.

Conclusion

The peculiar history of Ireland has ensured that many country houses have joined the abbeys, friaries, and castles as ruins in the melancholy countryside (another example is Castle ffogarty, Thurles, Co Tipperary, an insubstantial, rather papery Gothic pile, burnt in 1922, the ruins of which lurk eerily among the woods). However, even grand Classical houses (like Carton, Maynooth, Co Kildare, enlarged by architects of the stature of Cassels, Morrison, and others) have not fared well, and Carton itself has been threatened with development at various times. Emo Court, Portarlington, Co Leix, the only country house designed by the great James Gandon (1743-1823), himself a pupil of Sir William Chambers (1723-96 – architect of the exquisite Casino at Marino, near Dublin [1758-76]), has had a chequered history too. It was altered by Lewis Vulliamy (1791-1871), who added the Ionic portico to the garden-front in 1834-6. The Williamson Brothers (who designed The Argory, mentioned above) assisted Vulliamy on designs for the interiors. Emo Court was sold as a seminary in 1930, but returned to private hands in 1969, when the works of restoration were under Sir Albert Richardson's firm (Sir Albert himself having died by then). Powerscourt, Enniskerry, Co Wicklow (1731-40), was possibly Ireland's most celebrated country house, designed by Richard Cassels, in which German Baroque and English Palladian influences merged in an extraordinary whole. Later works were carried out under the direction of Sir

Mussenden Temple, Co Londonderry.

Richard Morrison, and from 1842 Daniel Robertson was also involved in the transformation of the terraces of the gardens into a grandly Italianate garden: Robertson precariously directed operations from a wheel-barrow (he had gout, and had difficulty in walking) in a state of sherry-induced inebriation. The central block of the house, with all its contents, was consumed by fire in the 1970s, a dreadful loss to the architectural heritage of Ireland but, unfortunately, nothing new.

Despite many catastrophes, however, Ireland still possesses a wealth of attractive houses. Many are still used as private dwellings, although a significant number have become hotels or institutions. What remains often delights, and even the melancholy ruins, crumbling and over-grown, often enhance the scenery. Certainly there is much in the way of stylistic variety, and not infrequently old fortified houses form part of later, more comfortable houses. But by far the greatest number of surviving houses are relatively unpreten-tious eighteenth- and nineteenth-century buildings, almost wholly innocent of fripperies or show, that, quite simply, look like what they were intended to be: the residences of gentlemen.

James Stevens Curl

Holywood, Co Down,

April 2002

ULSTER

Dunluce Castle

Bushmills, Co. Antrim

As you look along the coast, the white chalk cliffs are to the west, the Giant's Causeway to the east. The original mediaeval arch which controlled access to Dunluce Castle is lost, replaced by a gatehouse around 1600, with corbelled turrets of Scottish type.

The two-storied Great Hall, with tall (partially although unhistorically reconstructed) windows to the west, is a gracious building with finely moulded stones at parapet level which once supported the long-vanished roof. Beyond are kitchens and domestic quarters, parts of which fell into the sea in a disastrous collapse in 1639, taking some of the servants with it to a watery grave.

Left: Dunluce Castle, Co Antrim.

Beneath the north-eastern tower is a souterrain, the only remnant of a pre-castle fortification or dun (giving the castle a part of its name), which is said to date back to the Early Christian period. The oldest parts of the castle are the south wall and the two eastern towers, which date to the fourteenth century – by which period the place may already have been in the hands of the 'brave, hospitable and improvident' family of MacQuillans, who later relinquished it to the MacDonnells.

It was the MacDonnells who were responsible for building much of the remainder of the castle, including the service buildings on the mainland which funnelled visitors to the castle itself. After

Sir John Perrot, the English Lord Deputy, succeeded in taking the castle with the help of artillery in 1584, it subsequently reverted to the MacDonnells who then went on to give the castle its final shape, which we see in partial ruin today. The Spanish Armada galleon *Girona* was wrecked close to the castle in 1588, and Sir James MacDonnell succeeded in raising some of its cannons (now lost). But much of its remaining cargo was successfully salvaged in the 1960s, and is now prominently displayed in the Ulster Museum in Belfast.

Dunluce is one of Ireland's most spectacularly sited castles, perched on a rock connected to the mainland by a modern wooden bridge, formerly by a drawbridge.

Carrickfergus Castle

Carrickfergus, Co Antrim
Standing on a rocky spur above the harbour, Carrickfergus is the largest Anglo-Norman castle in Northern Ireland. Its core, the oldest part, is the inner ward and massive four-storey keep, entered at first-

floor level. Dating from the twelfth century, it was probably constructed by John de Courcy in the years after his initial conquest of Ulster in 1177. Attached to its southern flank was a walled courtyard, entered from the east by a gateway through which visitors to the castle had to pass. Within this courtyard was a large hall, remnants of which still survive. When King John came to Ireland in 1210, he captured the castle and, after his departure, the castle was further fortified by the addition of an outer wall defended by a strong square tower on the vulnerable eastern flank, which also gave cover to a new entrance north of the keep. Just to the north of this entrance there was a gully in the rock, which formed a natural defence, and between 1226 and 1242 the remainder of the rock-spur to the north of the gulley, originally unfortified, was enclosed by a wall entered through a massive gatehouse with two round towers. These portly towers with their portcullis guard the entrance for modern visitors (who, unlike their mediaeval counterparts, can gain entrance by paying a charge).

Left: Dunluce Castle, Co Antrim.

41

During the late Middle Ages, the castle played a purely administrative role, and only saw action again in 1689, when Schomberg took it for King William, who landed in Ireland here the following year. Its final, unsuccessful defence was against the French commander, Thurot, who succeeded in seizing it in 1760. Subsequently, it acted in turn as a prison, magazine, and armoury, and served as an air-raid shelter during the Second World War. The cannons which can be seen on its walls date partly from the seventeenth century, and partly from the early nineteenth century, when the castle was provided with new weaponry to guard against the threat of a Napoleonic invasion.

The town which grew up on the mainland under the protection of the castle was small and fortified by town walls. Carrickfergus, literally 'Rock of Fergus' recalls King Fergus MacErc, who was shipwrecked off the town c.320. More recent records reveal how the size of both town and walls was virtually doubled by Arthur Chichester in the early seventeenth century. William Congreve,

Carrickfergus Castle, Co Antrim.

Laurence Sterne, and more recently, Louis MacNeice all spent part of their childhood here. The walls are best seen from the outside in the north-eastern sector, at the car park next to the modern bowling green. On the western side, outside which the Scots and Irish lived, parts of the walls were exposed in excavations conducted in the 1970s. Within the walls is one of Ulster's most interesting churches, going back to the late twelfth century – St. Nicholas, with a

Interior of Carrickfergus Castle, Co Antrim.

late twelfth-century arcade, very rare in Ulster. Though founded probably by John de Courcy shortly before 1200, its present form dates partly from a rebuilding of 1614, and it contains the fine seventeenth-century tomb of Arthur Chichester in the north transept, which he himself had added. Carrickfergus, possesses one of Ireland's most impressive fortifications to survive from the Norman period.

Castle Ward

Strangford, Co Down

This fine but eccentric mansion was built by an unknown architect for the first Lord Bangor and his wife, Lady Anne, between *c.*1762-68. They could not agree upon the architectural style of the house. He preferred the Classical idiom so the south front was constructed of Bath stone, brought from Bristol in his own ships; she favoured the then-fashionable Gothic. There was no compromise, and the north front reflects the Strawberry Hill style.

This division of styles runs right through the house; with the saloon, library, and boudoir with its spectacular fan vaulting being Gothic, while the hall, dining room and staircase are in the Classical style.

Left: The Gothic Saloon at Castle Ward has an ogee Gothic mantel. The ceiling and cornice are also embellished with Gothic ornament.

Caledon Mansion

Caledon, Co Tyrone

The village of Caledon takes its name from the Earls of Caledon. Their mansion, (designed by Thomas Cooley in 1779 and enlarged by John Nash in 1810), is the fourth great house to be built here. It has a beautiful Regency drawing room and library, and the 4th Earl kept black bears in the park. On the estate is the ruin of a strange folly made out of of cattle bones. It was built in the eighteenth century and supposed to 'strike the Caledonians with wonder and amazement'. The butchers and tanners of Tyrone supplied the bones, though their opinions of the 'bone house' do not appear to have been recorded.

Enniskillen Castle

Enniskillen, Co Fermanagh

In a series of battles between the Maguires and the O'Neills on the one hand, and between the Maguires and the English on the other, the castle changed hands many times during the course of the sixteenth century. In 1602 it was taken by Niall Garve O'Donnell and the English, and five years later it was occupied solely by the English. The bottom of the tower (known as the keep) at the centre of the castle may be part of the original fifteenth century Maguire castle, but the remainder of the tower is the result of a later rebuild, and now houses a regimental museum. Standing on the river side of the enclosure is the 'water-gate', a twin-turreted building built probably in 1611. Much of the remaining sides of the enclosure are occupied by eighteenth- and nineteenth-century barrack buildings.

Enniskillen was awarded to Sir William Cole (d.1653), a Cornish planter and ancestor of the Earls of Enniskillen, following the confiscation of land after Tyrone's rebellion against the Crown forces. He settled there with twenty English families, defending it in 1641, when the castle was burned.

Right: Enniskillen Castle viewed from Lough Erne.

Malone House

Belfast, Co Antrim

Built during the 1820s for William Wallace Legge, a prominent Belfast merchant, the reconstructed house has stood in lands little changed for over a century and a half. The estate that was planted shortly after the house was built now supports a heritage of magnificent mature trees and woodland.

Bellamont Forest

Cootehill, Co Cavan

Bellamont Forest was designed by Sir Edward Lovett Pearce for the Cootes, Earls of Bellamont, around 1730. The family were descended from a brilliant soldier, Sir Thomas Coote, who was killed in 1642 'in a skirmish with the Irish'. His four sons were given land in different parts of Ireland – Sligo, Laois, Monaghan and Cavan – giving rise to the legend that you could walk across the country from one coast to the other without leaving Coote land.

Designed *c.*1730 by Sir Edward Lovett Pearce, the house is one of the finest examples of Palladian architecture in Ireland. Loosely based on Palladio's Villa Pisani, the house stands four-square on rising ground. It is constructed in red brick with a Doric limestone portico and pediments over the windows to either side. The entrance hall is particularly striking, with the simplicity of its black and white paved floor and marble busts of Roman emperors.

The house is private, but the grounds are accessible from the town and offer some pleasant walks. The town gets its name from the marriage of Thomas Coote, a colonel in the Crown forces, to Frances Hill of Hillsborough.

Derrymore House

Bessbrook, Co Armagh

Derrymore House, a delightful eighteenth-century thatched cottage ornée-style manor house, just outside the village, was built for Isaac Corry (1755-1813), MP, and last Chancellor of the Irish Exchequer. As Chancellor, he imposed the window tax, was involved in a number of duels (with pistols), and supported union between Ireland and Britain. He was a friend of Lord Castlereagh, and the Act of Union was drafted in the pretty drawing room in 1800.

Glebe House

Churchill, Letterkenny, Co Donegal

This Regency house, long the home of the artist Derek Hill, and donated to the State in 1981, is set in woodland gardens beside Lough Gartan. The work on display includes William Morris wallpapers and textiles, Islamic and Japanese art. The Derek Hill permanent collection includes 300 works by leading twentieth-century artists, including Picasso, Kokoshka, Morandi, and Sidney Nolan as well as Irish artists. Exhibitions are shown in the adjoining gallery.

Ardress House

Annaghmore, Co Armagh

The central portion of Ardress, behind the five centre windows of the front façade, is a two-storey gable-ended house built sometime around 1664 for the Clarke family. Internally the house retains its tripartite plan, with a long, narrow hall flanked by the parlour on the left and the former kitchen to the right.

Ardress, originally a modest farmhouse, was gradually transformed into a little mansion after the architect, George Ensor, married Sarah Clarke of Ardress in 1760. The drawing room was decorated by Michael Stapelton, a leading plasterer form Dublin. There are excellent examples of eighteenth-century furniture in the house, and a good collection of paintings.

The farmyard and outbuildings show aspects of farming history with a display of farm implements. There is a pleasant garden with examples of early types of Irish rose. The Ladies' Mile is a woodland walk around the estate.

The house was sold to the National Trust in 1960 who upgraded Ardress and restored the farmyard.

Overleaf: Ardress House, Annaghmore, Co Armagh.

Interior of Ardress House, Annaghmore, Co Armagh.

Mount Stewart

Newtownards, Co Down

The western end of the present house was built in 1804 for Robert Stewart, later first Marquess of Londonderry. It was designed by the celebrated London architect, George Dance. Modest in scale, the house was later enlarged by William Vitruvius Morrison, whilst keeping the original house intact. The main feature of the Morrison extension is a vast central hall with an octagonal gallery lit from above.

Charles, 3rd Marquess of Londonderry, and his wife Frances became celebrated figures, leading a glittering social life and travelling extensively. They collected works of art and furniture on their travels and brought them back to Mount Stewart. Among their more spectacular acquisitions were the 22 chairs used by delegates to the Congress of Vienna (where, in 1815, an attempt to settle peace in Europe was made). Each chair has been embroidered with the coat of arms of one of the delegates and the country he represented. Among the delegates were Talleyrand and Wellington. Lord Castlereagh used the chairs in his dining room, ranged beneath life-sized family portraits by Sir Godfrey Kneller. There is also a Stubbs painting of the racehorse Hambletonian – arguably the most important sporting picture in Ireland.

Mount Stewart offers the visitor one of the most complete gardens in the care of the National Trust. Designed by Edith, Lady Londonderry, from 1921, it encompasses almost every style of gardening, including a very beautiful burial-ground which is set on a height within the grounds.

When King Edward and Queen Alexandra visited the house in 1903 their hostess, the 6th Marchioness, had 274 servants to keep the royal guests happy. Even today, the family continue to live there, though the property is now owned by the National Trust.

Left: Interior of Mount Stewart House.
Following three pages: Mount Stewart House, its gardens, and dining-room.
The Mount Stewart estate has been designated a World Heritage site.

Florence Court

Enniskillen, Co Fermanagh

One of the most important Neo-Classical eighteenth-century buildings in the country, the building's early appearance is conjectural, but its basement was evidently retained for the present house, which was erected some time during the 1750s.

It was named after Florence Bourchier-Wrey, who married John Cole in 1707. The property was inherited by their son, who was elevated to the Irish peerage as Baron Mountflorence in 1760. The present mansion dates from 1751-64, with wings added some years later by Davis Ducart. The finely proportioned central block is flanked by arcades with end pavilions and the interior contains a set of state rooms prepared for a visit of George IV in 1821. These are decorated with Rococo plasterwork by John West.

The vigorous baroque treatment of the exterior is echoed in the large stone-flagged hall with its triglyph frieze, banded pilasters, pedimented door-case, massive Doric sandstone chimney-piece and linen-swag panels.

Visitors who look closely at the dining-room ceiling will notice some of the small holes drilled during the 1955 fire to allow the water pumped into the room above to drain away. These holes were the result of quick thinking on the part of the late Duchess of Westminster, Viola Grosvenor, who arrived during the fire to find little urgency about saving family treasures and discovered the old butler on the stairs removing a pair of his master's socks.

The National Trust acquired Florence Court as a gift in 1954 from John Henry Cole, 5th Earl of Enniskillen (1876-1963). The Trust has since successfully refurnished the building through donations and bequests. The emphasis has been on acquiring eighteenth-century Irish furniture. The extensive gardens (700 acres) contain numerous fine trees including the

Left: Florence Court, Enniskillen, Co Fermanagh.

parent tree from which the Florence Court Yew has been propagated.

Kilclief Tower-House

Strangford, Co Down

Overlooking the sea entrance to Strangford Lough, Kilclief is one of the finest of the many tower-houses dotted around the coast of Co Down. It was built as a manorial residence for the Bishops of Down, and is attributed to John Sely who became bishop in 1413 (he was deprived of his See in 1443, for having lived in the castle with a married woman). If the date is correct, this would make Kilclief the oldest surviving tower-house in Ireland. It was garrisoned for the Crown by Nicholas Fitzsymon and ten warders in 1601-2. The entrance to the four-storey tower was on the east side, protected by two flanking towers which are joined by an arch beneath the parapet level. The ground floor is roofed by a stone vault.

Springhill

Moneymore, Co Londonderry

When 'Good' Will Conyngham married Anne Upton in 1680 the marriage articles required him to build 'a convenient house of lime and stone, two stories high with the necessary office houses'. He built a tall, roofed house to which wings were added in the middle of the eighteenth century. Will was a soldier who played an important part in the defence of Derry in 1689 and his blunderbuss, flintlocks, and other firearms still hang in the gunroom. The family lived at Springhill for 300 years until Captain William Lenox-Conyngham left the house and its contents to the National Trust in 1957. It is set in attractive gardens and parkland. There is also an excellent collection of eighteenth- and nineteenth-costumes on display.

Mussenden Temple

Downhill, Co Londonderry

The temple, an elegant Classical rotunda, was designed by the Cork-born architect, Michael Shanahan in 1785 for Frederick Hervey, Earl of Bristol and Bishop of Derry. The Earl Bishop named it after his cousin, Mrs Mussenden, who died aged 22, just before its completion. Less prejudiced than many of his contemporaries, the Anglican

Mussenden Temple, Downhill, Co Londonderry.

bishop allowed a Catholic priest to celebrate Mass here once a week, as there was no local Catholic parish-church.

The Argory

Moy, Co Armagh

Overlooking the Blackwater river and set in wooded countryside, this handsome 1820 Classical mansion has remained unchanged since the early 1900s. It is still lit by acetylene gas, installed in 1906 by the Sunbeam Acetylene Gas Company of Belfast, and is said to be the only example surviving in the British Isles. The cluttered interiors evoke the Bond family's Edwardian taste and interests, and include a barrel-organ that is played once a month for musical house-tours. The beautiful estate offers garden, woodland, and riverside walks.

65

Donegal Castle

Donegal Town, Donegal

Donegal Castle was the residence of the O'Donnell Chiefs. From 1593 until his death in 1602 Red Hugh O'Donnell, Lord of Tirconnell, in alliance with Hugh O'Neill, Earl of Tyrone, fought English armies in the Nine Years War. After the submission of the Ulster Lords to King James I and VI in 1603 the castle remained in O'Donnell hands for a few more years, but after the Flight of the Earls in 1607 and the subsequent confiscation of property held by the O'Donnells and O'Neills (among other Irish Lords), the castle was granted to an Englishman, Sir Basil Brooke, who rebuilt it. The castle still has the original tower built by the O'Donnells, but Brooke added a fine Jacobean five-bay, three-storey gabled manor house, and also replaced the upper slit windows of the keep with stone mullioned windows and roof gables.

Donegal Castle, Donegal Town, Donegal.

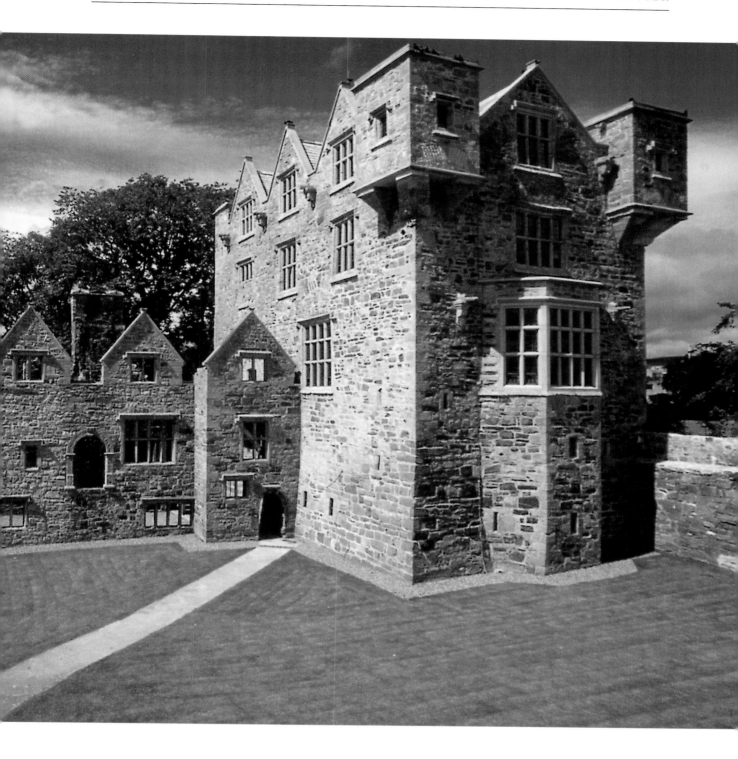

Ardglass Jordan's and Cowd Castle

Ardglass, Co Down

Ardglass contains more mediaeval tower-houses than any other town in Ireland, reflecting its importance as Ulster's busiest port in the fifteenth century.

Jordan's Castle was probably built in the fifteenth century and, like others of its kind, was a fortified family residence, owned by the Jordan family. Simon Jordan is celebrated for having defended the castle for three years during the Tyrone Rebellion until relieved by the Lord Deputy, Mountjoy, in 1601.

Jordan's Castle is a three-storey tower with attic floor above, and with the north door protected by projecting towers. The Belfast solicitor Francis Joseph Bigger bought the castle in 1911, restored it and subsequently bequeathed it to the State.

Smaller in scale is another of the Ardglass tower-houses in state care: Cowd Castle, a hundred metres to the south-east, which has two floors and an attic, both with floors of wood. It stands today in the grounds of a golf course, whose clubhouse preserves substantial remains of fifteenth-century warehouses.

Dundrum Castle

Dundrum, Co Down

Dundrum is one of the finest Norman castles in Northern Ireland. It was built by John de Courcy in the last decades of the twelfth century and first mentioned in the historical records when it was unsuccessfully besieged in 1205, and taken by King John five years later.

The upper of the two wards, on the top of the commanding hiss, is dominated by a tall, round keep or donjon with immensely thick walls, from the top of which a splendid view may be had over the sea and the south of Co Down. This upper ward is protected by a rock-cut ditch and an extensive curtain-wall entered from the south, where two

Overleaf: Dundrum castle, Dundrum, Co Down.

towers (one with a semicircular bastion) guard the entrance, which overlooks the lower ward now containing the shell of a seventeenth-century house. The castle passed through the hands of the Earl of Ulster in 1227 to the Magennis family, which occupied it in the later Middle Ages.

Castle Coole

Enniskillen, Co Fermanagh

Arguably the finest Neo-Classical country seat in Ireland, Castle Coole was completed in 1797, for the then Earl of Belmore. As he advanced in the peerage he may have wanted to equal the grandeur of the home of his brother-in-law and neighbour, the Earl of Enniskillen, at Florence Court. The house cost twice the estimated £30,000 to build. The attention to detail is superb – the plasterer had worked for Robert Adam at both Syon House and Harewood House in England.

Lord Belmore died leaving huge debts. The second Earl employed a leading Dublin upholsterer to furnish Castle Coole in the Regency style. Tassles, sumptuous wall-hangings, and gilded furniture abounded. Many items of furniture had two or three protective covers, and one pair of scarlet silk curtains cost £1,000 for the material alone.

The remains of an oak avenue can be seen in the park, and the lake is famous for having the oldest flock of non-migratory greylag geese in the British Isles. Introduced by James Corry around 1700, legend has it that if they leave Castle Coole, so will the Lowry-Corrys. The National Trust has owned Castle Coole since 1951.

Barons Court

Newtownstewart, Co Tyrone

Surrounded by oak trees and three lakes, Barons Court, the seat of the Dukes of Abercorn, was originally designed by George Steuart, a Gaelic speaker from the north of Scotland who is best known for having designed Attingham Hall in Shropshire in 1783. However, when the

property was inherited by John James Hamilton (he would become known in the family and to everyone else as the 'Old Marquess'), Sir John Soane revamped parts of the interior, and a major refurbishment was carried out under the direction of W.V. Morrison in the 1830s. The rotunda is at the heart of the house. Once used for billiards, it has since been transformed into a dining room. It is lit from above (there are no windows), the domed and coffered ceiling supported by a ring of Ionic columns.

Ballywalter Park

Ballywalter, Co Down

Ballywalter was aptly described by Professor Alistair Rowan as 'a building with a metropolitan air and all the architectural trappings of a London club.' Built for Andrew Mulholland, the Mayor of Belfast, in 1846, the house is the most complete example of a nineteenth-century Italianate *palazzo* in Ireland. The staircase hall is stunning: the staircase is of white marble, lit by a stained-glass dome, with a colonnade of columns forming a loggia at the top.

Harry Avery's Castle

Newtownstewart, Co Tyrone

The Harry Avery who gave his name to the castle was Henry Aimbreidh O'Neill, who died in 1392. The castle, commanding the valley of the River Derg close to Newtownstewart, was probably built by him, and is unusual in being a stone castle located within what was Gaelic Ulster at the time. The two towers, visible from afar, give the impression of being a gate-tower of an earlier century, guarding access to the castle ward behind them. The entrance leads into a covered hall where a staircase once rose to the main living area at first-floor level, so that the towers seem to have functioned more as a tower-house than as a fortified gate. The area behind the towers was protected by a curtain wall, in which traces of one latrine tower may still be seen.

Tully Castle

Church Hill, Co Donegal

Tully Castle is beautifully sited on a hill overlooking the west shore of lower Lough

Harry Avery's Castle, Newtownstewart, Co Tyrone.

Erne. It was built by a Scottish planter, Sir John Hume, with strong defensive 'bawn' walls around it in 1610-13. Historically it is a 'time capsule', as it was lived in for just thirty years before its horrific end.

When Sir John died, his son Sir George inherited the castle. But in 1641, as part of the great uprising at that time, Roderick Maguire, the local chief, seized the castle. The garrison surrendered, but only under promise of safe conduct to Enniskillen. Maguire then burnt the castle down and massacred everyone around – some 75 people. For 350 years it lay ruined and desolate. When the site was cleared of ivy and growth in the 1970s, the paths of an old garden were found inside the bawn, and an authentic seventeenth-century style garden has been recreated.

73

Glenveagh Castle

Letterkenny, Co Donegal

Glenveagh Castle consists of a four-storey keep and was designed by JT Trench in 1870 for Mr Adair and his wife, the American heiress Cornelia Wadworth. It was built as a romantic shooting box and it was here that royalty were entertained.

The castle is surrounded by one of the finest gardens in Ireland, which contrast with the rugged surroundings of some 40,000 acres of mountains, lakes, glens and woods. A herd of red deer grazes nearby.

The whole property is now managed as a National Park, and is visited by more than 90,000 people each year.

Glenveagh Castle, Letterkenny, Co Donegal.

Belfast Castle

Belfast, Co Antrim

A 'Belfast Castle' has been on this site since the twelfth century. The Chichesters (later the Donegalls) lived in England as absentee landlords but came to live at Ormeau at the beginning of the nineteenth century. The present building was designed by John Lanyon in the Scottish Baronial style, popularised some years earlier by the reconstruction of Balmoral Castle in 1853.

The building was completed in 1870, having far exceeded the initial estimate of £11,000. The Donegall fortune had dwindled so drastically that the project was nearly left unfinished. The Donegall coat of arms appears over the front door and on the north wall of the castle, while a section of the Shaftesbury crest appears on the exterior staircase. The family presented the castle and estate to the City of Belfast in 1934.

Belfast Castle, Belfast, Co Antrim.

LEINSTER

Emo Court

Portarlington, Co Laois

A magnificent Neo-Classical house designed by James Gandon in 1790, on the same magnificent scale as his Custom House, was built for John Dawson, 1st Earl of Portarlington. The construction began in 1790 and additions were made at different stages. The fashionable English architect Lewis Vulliamy added the north front portico with four giant Ionic columns in 1834.

The domed rotunda at Emo Court, inspired by the Roman Pantheon, must surely be one of the most impressive rooms in Ireland. The circular space is lit by a lantern in the coffered dome, which rests on the gilded capitals and Sienna marble pilasters. The house is surrounded by extensive parklands with formal lawns, a lake and woodland walks.

Ballyfin House

Ballyfin, Co Laois

Ballyfin House is possibly the finest Neo-Classical houses in the country. It was built in 1821-6 in Slieve Bloom sandstone by Sir Charles Coote, to the designs first of Dominic Madden (best known for Tuam Cathedral) and then Sir Richard Morrison and his son William Vitruvius. On entering

Left: Dublin Castle, Dublin, Co Dublin.
Overleaf: Emo Court, Portarlington, Co Laois.

by the tetrastyle Ionic portico and through the formal entrance hall, one is confronted by a magnificent suite of rooms. Adjoining the library is a superb Richard Turner conservatory. The grounds were landscaped by Sutherland and include fine trees, vistas, ice caves, a grotto, a serpentine lake, a tower folly, and three gatelodges.

Newbridge House

Donabate, Co Dublin

This eighteenth-century manor is set on 350 acres of parkland, twelve miles north of the city centre. It has one of the finest Georgian interiors in Ireland. The house, designed by George Semple, was built in 1737 for Charles Cobbe, later Archbishop of Dublin. It contains elaborate stucco plasterwork by Robert West.

In 1760 the Archbishop's fashionable daughter-in-law, Lady Elizabeth Beresford,

added a large wing to the back of the Classical mansion containing the magnificent red drawing room. A fine example of a Georgian room, it was designed to display her husband's collection of seventeenth- and eighteenth-century paintings. The crimson damask wall covering and the co-ordinating carpet and curtains date back 170 years.

The unique museum of curiosities dating back to 1790 is full of fascinating objects brought back by the widely travelled Cobbes, and displayed in specially designed cabinets.

Newman House

Dublin, Co Dublin

Two Georgian houses located on St Stephen's Green, Nos 85 and 86, contain examples of Dublin's finest eighteenth-century plasterwork. Built as the townhouses of two wealthy Irish landowners, the houses are both stone-faced, and are richly ornamented with spectacular plasterwork walls and ceilings. Though less than thirty years apart, (begun in 1738 and 1765 respectively), these buildings vividly illustrate the dramatic development in Irish stucco from the later Baroque style to fully-fledged Irish Rococo. No other building offers such a complete and satisfying experience of Irish Georgian stucco work.

The unique union of an early Georgian townhouse and a later Georgian residence was brought about in the Victorian period when both houses were acquired by the Catholic University of Ireland, the precursor of today's University College Dublin. The building is named in honour of the University's first rector Cardinal John Henry Newman.

Castletown House

Celbridge, Co Kildare

Castletown is the largest and most significant Palladian-style country house in Ireland. It was built *c.*1722 for the speaker of the Irish House of Commons, William Conolly (1622-1729), the son of a Donegal innkeeper who, through astute dealings in forfeited estates after the Williamite wars, became one of the richest men in Ireland.

The designs of a number of important architects were used, notably Alessandro Galilei (who is best known for his work on the Lateran Basilica in Rome), Sir Edward Lovett Pearce, and later Sir William Chambers.

It is not known precisely how much of Castletown is Galilei's work, but he was certainly responsible for devising the

Overleaf: Castletown House, Celbridge, Co Kildare.

overall scheme of the centre block, which was flanked by colonnades to lower service pavilions in the manner of Palladio's villas in the Veneto – a concept that was completely new in Ireland and later became the prototype and inspiration for numerous houses.

Plasterwork of 1759-60 by the Lafranchini brothers embellishes the walls of the slightly later cantilevered staircase, with brass banisters. The Long Gallery on the first floor is decorated in the style of an actual wall painting discovered during the excavation of Pompeii, and is the work of Thomas Riley. Also noteworthy is the 'print room' papered with eighteenth-century engravings by Lady Louisa Conolly (*c.*1770), the only one to survive in Ireland.

It remained in the Conolly family until 1965. Saved from demolition, the empty and abandoned house and some parkland was bought by the Honourable Desmond Guinness. The house became the headquarters of the Irish Georgian Society which undertook its restoration. It was taken into state care in 1994.

Duckett's Grove

Carlow, Co Carlow

The ruins of Co Carlow's finest Gothic mansion, the house was destroyed by fire in 1933. The eponymous home of the Duckett family from the middle of the seventeenth century until 1915, an imposing gate lodge still remains.

Carlow Castle

Carlow, Co Carlow

The castle, probably built by William the Marshall c.1208, is the earliest of the typical Anglo Norman four tower keeps. It was built to defend the River Barrow, the prontier of the Pale. Attacked on numerous occasions, the castle survived until 1814, when a Dr. Middleton attempted to convert it into a lunatic asylum.. using an excessive charge of gunpower to remoe some of the interior, he succeded in demolishing three quarters of the stucture. Only the west wall of the keep and two of its former towers are now remaining.

Huntington Castle

Clonegal, Co Carlow

The old core of Huntington Castle is a tower-house built by Laurence, first and last Lord Esmonde between 1625 and 1630. Its three-storey four-bay castellated front seems hardly to have a straight line anywhere – the side walls gently lean at an angle and the sash windows lie askew. The castle remained largely unaltered until 1849 when the property was inherited by Alexander Durdin whose grand-uncle had married the two daughters and co-heirs of Sir John Esmond, third Baronet, as his two successive wives.

Huntington was one of the first country houses in Ireland to have electricity, and in order to satisfy local interest a light was kept burning on the front lawn so that the curious could come up and inspect it. It is said to be haunted, and there is even a temple to the Goddess Isis in the castle.

Belvedere

Mullingar, Co Westmeath

Belvedere was built around 1740 to a design by Richard Castle, probably as a fishing pavilion, for Robert Rochfort MP, (later created Earl of Belvedere,) whose seat at Gaulston lay five miles away. Although its rooms are now empty, Belvedere remains much as it was in the Earl's time. A solid grey limestone house of two stories over a basement with a long front and curved end bows, it is probably the earliest bow-ended house in the country.

The delicate Rococo plasterwork ceilings are the real glory of Belvedere's interior, and are worth a visit for their own sake. Framed by rich cornices, these ceilings are notable for their lively quality and freedom of movement. They have been attributed to Bartholomew Cramillion.

The small park that Lord Belvedere created around his villa is just as fine as the house itself, and was the envy of all visitors. However, the view south is blocked by the remarkable and vindictively named Jealous Wall, the largest Gothic folly in Ireland. This was built to screen from view the house of Lord Belevedere's brother, with whom he had had a severe quarrel.

Edgeworthstown

Edgeworthstown, Co Longford

The Edgeworth family became established in the neighbourhood in 1583, when the first Irish Edgeworth was appointed Bishop of Down and Connor. The eighteenth-century house was built by Richard Lovell Edgeworth (1744-1817), who was a benefactor to the village, an improving landlord, inventor and father to twenty-two children.

Among his children was Maria Edgeworth (1767-1849) who taught school in the upstairs room. After the publication of her satirical Anglo-Irish novel 'Castle Rackrent', she had many distinguished visitors such as Sir Walter Scott and William Wordsworth, who acknowledged her influence. The house was occupied by the Edgeworth Family until 1935, when it was purchased by Mr Noonan who donated the house and fifty acres to the Sisters of Mercy.

Ardagh House

Ardagh, Co Longford

Lady Fetherstone's ancestral home was Ardagh House, a manor house, situated to the north of the village and now a convent. It was here, it is fabled, that a young Oliver Goldsmith swaggered and bragged in the mistaken belief that he had arrived at an inn. The landlord humoured him for the night, but Goldsmith's dismay on realising his mistake the following morning can easily be imagined. However, he later turned his embarrassment to his advantage, the incident being central to his comedy 'She Stoops to Conquer', which was first performed in 1773.

Carrigglas Manor

Longford, Co Longford

This romantic house designed by Daniel Robertson of Scotland in the Tudor-Gothic Revival style, looks like the perfect setting for an early nineteenth-century novel. And there is in fact a literary connection. An earlier house belonging to the banking Newcomen family was rebuilt by Daniel Robertson for Thomas Lefroy, Lord Chief Justice of Ireland in 1837. When a young man studying in England, Lefroy become an inamorato of Jane Austen. It is believed that he was the inspiration for Mr Darcy in 'Pride and Prejudice'.

The beautifully restored interiors of the house have some charming plasterwork ceilings, with appropriate symbolism: grapes and vines – the symbol of a good table – in the dining-room; oak leaves for wisdom in the library; and roses and lilies in the drawing-room. The magnificent stable yard designed by James Gandon in 1790 (architect of the Custom House and Four Courts), is the only surviving example of his agricultural work, and now houses a fascinating costume and lace museum.

Interior of Russborough, Blessington, Co Wicklow.

Avondale House

Rathdrum, Co Wicklow

Avondale House, possibly designed by Wyatt, and built by Samuel Hayes in *c*.1779, passed to the Parnell family in 1795. It was at Avondale on 27 June 1846 that one of the greatest political leaders of modern Irish history, Charles Stewart Parnell, was born. The house now is a museum to his memory, and a major refurbishment programme has restored much of the house to its decor of 1850.

Russborough

Blessington, Co Wicklow

Russborough was designed by Richard Castle for Joseph Leeson, first Earl of Milltown. The building of the house began about 1741 and took nearly ten years to complete. The house is built of granite in the Palladian style. The front façade has a fine flight of steps, with heraldic lions and urns, a sweep of graceful curved colonnades crowned on the skyline with Baroque urns, and well-proportioned, solid flanking wings. It has fine examples of plasterwork by the Lafrancini brothers and was described in 1948 as 'a noble new house forming into perfection'.

Alfred Beit, uncle of the present owner, founded the De Beer Diamond Mining Company at Kimberley with Cecil Rhodes, and started collecting works of art in the 1880s. Sir Alfred Beit acquired the house in 1951, and it now accommodates the treasures of the Beit Foundation. The house also contains magnificent displays of silver, bronzes, porcelain, fine furniture, tapestries, and carpets.

Killruddery House

Bray, Co Wicklow

In 1618 the land where Killruddery stands, situated at the front of the Little Sugar Loaf Mountain, was granted to Sir William Brabazon, created Earl of Meath in 1627. However, the original house was destroyed and later rebuilt by the second Earl in 1651. There is a delightful eighteenth-century

*Killruddery House,
Bray, Co Wicklow.*

93

painting in the library at Killruddery of seventeenth-century huntsmen galloping beyond the formal gardens. These gardens have miraculously survived – a rare and enchanting example of Baroque landscaping on a grand scale.

The most important early features are the 'angles', radiating hedges of beech and hornbeam with statuary at the centre, long double canals mirroring the parkland and a circular pond and fountain surrounded by a giant beech hedge. Later additions include a sylvan theatre, a parterre, a collection of statuary and a fine Victorian conservatory in the manner of the Crystal Palace, London. In 1820 the 10th Earl of Meath made extensive alterations to the house, employing the then fashionable architects Richard and William Morrison. They remodelled the house creating a Neo-Tudor edifice, an excellent example of its kind but immense in scale and therefore impossible to heat. In 1953 the present Earl commissioned the architect Claud Phillimore to reduce the house to its present more manageable proportions. Both the large and small drawing rooms have particularly fine plasterwork ceilings.

Killincarrig Fortified House

Kilcoole, Co Wicklow

One of the few surviving houses of the early seventeenth century in Ireland, this L-shaped house was the first to be taken by Cromwell on his march from Dublin to Wexford in 1649. On the ground floor it has a main hall with a fireplace, a kitchen at right angles and stairs in a tower projecting from one side of the hall. The house has twenty-three single- or double-mullioned windows, and two chimneys.

Powerscourt

Enniskerry, Co Wicklow

Powerscourt was built in 1731 by Richard Castle for the Wingfield family, Viscounts Powerscourt, incorporating the massive walls of the ancient castle of the De La Poers that stood on the site. Daniel Robertson designed its famous terraced gardens and round pond.

The house suffered a disastrous fire in 1974, just before it was due to be opened to the public, which destroyed many of its valuable contents and the whole of the top floor. It has now been restored.

Castletown

Piltown, Co Kilkenny

Known as Castletown 'Cox' to avoid confusion with Castletown in Co Kildare, this great house was built in 1767 for Michael Cox, Archbishop of Cashel. Designed by a Sardinian architect, Davis Ducart, the garden front with its giant fluted Corinthian pilasters and beautiful arcades, is spectacular.

All the ground-floor rooms, and the staircase, have rich Rococo plaster decoration by Patrick Osborne of Waterford. The Corinthian columns in the front hall are monoliths, each carved out of a single piece of limestone. The attractive formal box gardens were laid out in 1909. The design is one of overall perfection, and it is regarded as the finest small Palladian house in the country.

Kilkenny Castle

Kilkenny, Co Killenny

A twelfth-century castle built by William the Marshall, remodelled in Victorian times and set in extensive parklands – this was the principal seat of the Butler family, the Marquesses and Dukes of Ormonde.

Due to major restoration works, the central block now includes a library, drawing room, and bedrooms decorated in the full splendour of the 1830s, as well as the beautiful Long Gallery. There is a fine Classical gateway in the west wall dating to 1684, and a suite of former servants' rooms

Overleaf and following page: Kilkenny Castle, Kilkenny, Co Kilkenny.

is now the Butler Art Gallery, which mounts frequently changing art exhibitions.

Ballyhack Castle

Ballyhack, Co Wexford

Ballyhack Castle, a large tower-house, is thought to have been built *c.*1450 by the Knights Hospitallers of St John, one of the two great military orders founded in the twelfth century at the time of the Crusades. Located on a steep slope, the castle is in a commanding position overlooking the Waterford Estuary.

Tullynally Castle

Castlepollard, Co Westmeath

Tullynally Castle, formerly known as Pakenham Hall, is the seat of the Pakenhams, Earls of Longford. Several architects, Francis Johnston, Sir Richard Morrison, James Sheil, and J Rawson Carroll effected the transformation of the Classical house into a Gothic castle from 1803 onwards. The Gothic dining room has wallpaper designed by Pugin for the Houses of Parliament, hung with portraits of the family.

The castle has mementos of the Duke of Wellington, whose wife was Catherine Pakenham. It was also the home of Edward Longford (1902-61), the 7th Earl, who directed the Gate Theatre of Dublin which toured the provinces for many years, bringing European drama to country towns.

Trim Castle

Trim, Co Meath

Trim Castle is the largest Anglo-Norman castle in Ireland. Hugh de Lacy began construction of the castle in about 1172 but the central tower – the keep – was not completed until the 1220s. This twenty-sided tower is three stories high and was protected by a ditch, a curtain wall and a moat. Inside the tower were living quarters, a great hall and a small chapel.

The curtain wall was defended by five D-shaped towers and entry to the castle was only through either of the two gates. The Towngate had a portcullis to protect it as well as a 'murder hole'. The other gate, the Dublingate, has a barbican projecting from the tower. Originally, the barbican spanned the moat which surrounded the curtain wall and had a drawbridge, operated from above.

It was here that Richard de Burgh, Earl of Ulster, held court in the reign of Edward II. Richard II confined his cousins(Humphrey of Gloucester and Henry of Lancaster – afterwards Henry IV) in the castle because they were opposed to his attempt as monarch to exercise greater control.

Trim Castle, covering an area of three acres, has undergone extensive conservation work and has been recently opened to the public after many years.

Ferns Castle

Ferns, Co Wexford

The castle was built in the thirteenth century, on the site of the stronghold of the Kings of Leinster. Partially dismantled in 1641 by Sir Charles Coote,the castle originally ormed a square, with large corner towers. Only half of the castle is still standing. Of the remains, the most complete tower contains a fine circular chapel, with carved ornament. The tower also has several original fireplaces and a vaulted basement. Archeological excavations revealed a rock-cut ditch outside the castle walls.

Ferns Castle is one of a number of historic sites in Ferns. Others include St. Mary's; a twelfth-century Augustinian Priory; the remains of a thirteenth-century cathedral; a small nave-and-chancel church and some High Crosses and parts of crosses, which stand in the cathedral grounds.

Overleaf: Ferns Castle, Ferns, Co Wexford.

Marino Casino

Clontarf, Co Dublin

This Casino, which means 'small house', on the outskirts of Dublin, was designed by Sir William Chambers as an elaborate garden pavilion for the first Earl of Charlemont in 1758. It is one of the finest and original Franco-Roman Neo-Classical buildings in Europe.

Chambers brought Simon Vierpyl from Rome to do the stone-carving on the Casino, and Edward Smyth, the Irish sculptor, worked as his assistant. Joseph Wilton executed the lions, and Cipriani the panel beneath them. The carved decoration of the Casino is without parallel in Ireland for its richness and quality of the Classical ornament. After years of neglect and vandalism, the house was taken into state care in 1930 but regrettably it was not until 1974 that any major restoration took place.

Left: Marino Casino, Clontarf, Co Dublin.

Dublin Castle

Dublin, Co Dublin

Dublin Castle was originally built in the reign of King John (*c*.1205) as a 'citadel of defence and a place to deposit the Royal Treasure'. Later in the reign of Queen Elizabeth, (*c*.1560), its uses were extended to include the holding of Courts by the Lord Lieutenants, or Chief Governors of Ireland.

The first Lord Deputy to make his residence here was Sir Henry Sidney in 1565, and it remained the seat of the Lords Lieutenants until the establishment of the Irish Free State in 1922.

This Anglo-Norman fortress closely resembles other Norman Castles built throughout Ireland in the twelfth and thirteenth centuries. Like others, it has certain dominant characteristics – namely a large, open quadrilateral keep surrounded by a curtain wall, with massive circular drum towers at the corners and an entrance gateway protected by smaller D-shaped towers in one of the curtain walls. Dublin Castle initially had the added safeguard of a moat on the two sides exposed to attack. The moat was provided by the River Poddle, which still runs under the castle. The remaining two sides were within the city. The remains of all four towers and fragments of the walls can still be seen.

From the eighteenth century the castle's present appearance began to develop, through the work of Sir William Robinson and Frank Johnston and others. The State Apartments on one side of the Castle Yard, built as residence of the viceroy, include the spacious St Patrick's Hall. The painted ceiling and frieze bear the arms of the Knights of St Patrick. All Presidents of the Irish Republic are inaugurated here.

The Throne Room in the Castle is the place where English kings and queens received their subjects. The huge throne is thought to have been presented by William of Orange. The throne was last used in 1911 by George V.

Left: Dublin Castle, Dublin, Co Dublin.

Above, left and overleaf:
Dublin Castle, Dublin, Co Dublin.

*Left: Tullynally Castle,
Castlepollard, Co Westmeath.*

MUNSTER

Bunratty Castle

Co Clare

Bunratty Castle is the most complete mediaeval castle in Ireland. It was built *c.*1425, changing ownership and being plundered on many occasions. Acquired by Viscount Gort in 1956, it has been restored to how it would have appeared during the fifteenth or sixteenth century. It contains an important collection of antique furniture, as well as tapestries housed in the re-roofed banqueting hall above the stone-roofed guardroom.

Swiss Cottage

Cahir, Co Tipperary

About a mile south of the town, and built on a platform with a fine view over the River Suir, is the Swiss Cottage, a cottages ornés inspired by the consciously 'rural' buildings buildings erected for Queen Marie Antoinette of France at Versailles.

This example, said to be the 'finest cottage orné in the world', was built in 1810 for the young society couple, Richard Butler, Lord Cahir, and his wife Emily. They succeeded in attracting the well-known English architect, John Nash, to come to Ireland to design the building, which he followed two years later with the King's Cottage in Windsor Park. The Swiss Cottage, which got its sobriquet decades after it was built because of its resemblance to some Alpine homes, is a two-storey house which was given a new, superbly

Left: Bunratty Castle, Co Clare.
Overleaf: Swiss Cottage, Cahir, Co Tipperary.

executed roof of thatch in 1989-90, and provided at the same time with stick-work verandahs on the outside. Inside, the furniture and wallpaper, part original and part restoration, have been assembled with great flair and taste. The music room has original wallpaper depicting scenes on the Bosphorus.

Damer House

Roscrea, Co Tipperary

Joseph Damer of Tipperary was granted the town and lordship of Roscrea in 1722. He married two years later and shortly afterwards built an elegant townhouse within the curtain walls of the old castle.

Such arrangements were common, and later houses were often built beside or attached to the strongholds they replaced. The troubled state of the country meant that the Irish gentry found it wiser to live in castles or fortified tower-houses until the end of the seventeenth century.

Right: Damer House, Roscrea, Co Tipperary.

The house has a magnificent carved pine staircase, similar to the one at Cashel Palace. Another interesting feature is the scroll pedimented doorway. During most of the nineteenth century the building was used as a barracks. Restoration was carried out initially by the Irish Georgian Society and then by the Roscrea Heritage Society.

Mount Ievers Court

Sixmilebridge, Co Clare

Although Mount Ievers Court looks as if it was built around 1710, work did not in fact begin until *c.*1736-37, when Colonel Henry Ievers demolished the seventeenth-century tower-house that his grandfather Henry Ievers had acquired less than seventy years before. The architect were John and Issac Rothery

The entrance front is of ashlar stone, and the garden front of brick which has faded over the years to a shade of silvery pink. The interior of the house has a simple, restrained

feel. Many rooms retain their contemporary panelling, including several in plaster that directly follow the lines of wood panelling.

Other features include the fine brass knocker on the front door, the vaulted basements and a delightful 1740s fresco in the drawing room giving a panoramic view of the house, demesne and landscape beyond. The formal garden landscape around the house has now largely disappeared, although the fish-ponds have been restored.

Cratloe Woods House

Cratloe, Co Clare

The ghost of daring red-haired Maire Rua O'Brien is said to guard the driveway at Cratloe Woods House. But for her resourcefulness the O'Briens might have forfeited their lands to English settlers. To keep the estates, the widowed Maire agreed to marry an English army officer. Cratloe Woods was first lived in by her grandson, playboy Lucius O'Brien and his wife Catherine Keightly. The red-painted house dating to the seventeenth century is an example of an Irish longhouse. It remained in the ownership of the O'Briens (who built it and who traced their ancestry to the eleventh-century King of Ireland, Brian Boru) for almost three hundred years.

Muckross House

Killarney, Co Kerry

Muckross House was built in 1843. A magnificent Victorian mansion, it is one of Ireland's most important stately homes, set amidst the spectacular scenery of Killarney National Park. The fine, elegantly furnished rooms still give a sense of the lifestyle of the landed gentry even today, while below stairs are revealed the working conditions of the servants. Visitors to Muckross House can view skilled craft workers using traditional methods to produce high-quality items of weaving, bookbinding and pottery.

The gardens at Muckross are famed world-wide for their beauty. In particular they are noted for their fine collection of rhododendrons and azaleas, the water garden, and an outstanding rock garden hewn out of natural limestone.

Carrigaholt Tower

Shannon, Co Clare

This is a tall and slender five-storey tower standing in one corner of a bawn and built originally by the MacMahons, Lords of Corcabascin, around the end of the fifteenth century. It is beautifully situated overlooking the Shannon estuary and Carrigaholt pier.

The tower is complete with musket holes, (also known as 'murder holes') to drop things on intruders' heads when they came in the door, and it also has a vault on the fourth floor. Teige Caech 'The Short-sighted' Macmahon was unsuccessfully besieged in the tower by Sir

Overleaf: Muckross House, Killarney, Co Kerry.

Conyers Clifford in 1598, but a few months later the Earl of Thomond ucceeded in wrestling the castle from him. It was then taken over by Daniel O'Brien who built the fireplace on the fifth floor which bears the date 1603 (it seems likely that he was also the one who built many of the present windows into the tower).

In 1646, Admiral Sir William Penn called at the castle on his way to Kinsale, having just abandoned Bunratty to the Confederate troops. In 1651 it was taken by Cromwell's general, Ludlow, who kept a garrison there until 1652. Charles II, however, restored the castle to the O'Briens in 1666. But in 1691 William of Orange gave it to Keppel, Earl of Albermarle, who sold it almost immediately afterwards to the Burtons, who retained it up till the present century. The bawn protecting the tower is fairly well preserved, though the turret overlooking the pier is modern.

Blarney House

Blarney, Co Cork

The gabled and turreted Blarney House is one of the most elegant and gracious of the great houses of Ireland. Built in 1874, it is beautifully situated overlooking Blarney Lake. It contains a collection of early furniture, family portraits, tapestries and works of art.

Blarney Castle

Blarney, Co Cork

A large fifteenth-century castle built by Cormac Laidhir MacCarthy, Lord of Muskerry, on a rock overlooking the river Martin. It consists of a tall tower and a stouter and later battlemented keep. It is famous for the Blarney Stone, which is actually a sill of one of the machicolations of the castle.

The legend of the stone's properties is relatively modern. Difficult to reach, the 'stone' when kissed, is said to endow the speaker with extraordinary powers of eloquence. However the association with the name Blarney dates back to when MacCarthy tried to talk his way out of handing over Blarney Castle to an agent of Queen Elizabeth I. He prevaricated until the Queen declared 'I will hear no more of this Blarney talk.'

Fota Island

Carrigtwohill, Co Cork

Fota Island, is a Regency mansion. The existing house was enlarged and given a Regency flavour in 1825 by Sir Richard and William Vitruvius Morrison for the Smith-Barry family. Fota's former owners, the Smith-Barrys, were direct descendants of David de Barry, a Norman adventurer and later settler who was granted lands in Cork in 1179. The family's main castle was at Buttevant in Co Cork.

The exterior of the house is plain compared to the splendours of the interior.

Ornate plasterwork, typically Morrisonian, decorates the ceilings and wreaths alternate with the Barry crest in the frieze. The staircase, which has brass banisters, is cantilevered and has an oval domed ceiling.

In the 1840s James Hugh, John Smith-Barry's son, reclaimed the swampy land and created the famous arboretum, as well as water gardens and semi-tropical jungle.

Coppinger's Court

Cork, Co Cork

The ruins of a four-storey house consisting of a central block flanked by two fortified square blocks on the east side, and with another in the centre of the west side. There are some mullioned windows on the top floor on the western side, while there are well-preserved turrets on the southern side and at the north-western corner just below the parapets. The chimney stacks are well preserved.

Overleaf: Barryscourt Castle, Carrigtwohill, Co Cork.

The house was built by Sir Walter Coppinger, who surrendered his estates to James I in 1616 and had them regranted to him the following day.

Barryscourt Castle

Carrigtwohill, Co Cork

Barryscourt Castle was the seat of the Barry family from the twelfth to the seventeenth centuries. The present castle is a fine example of a fifteenth-century tower-house with sixteenth-century additions and alterations. The bawn wall with three corner towers is largely intact.

Dunkathel

Cork, Co Cork

Wealthy Cork merchant Abraham Morris chose an idyllic spot to build his house overlooking the River Lee. The architect is thought to be Abraham Hargrave of Cork, a pupil of Davis Ducart, who was responsible for some of the other fine properties of the area such as Lota and Kilshannig.

The house dates from around 1790 and has a finely proportioned interior with Adam chimney-pieces and a splendid bifurcated staircase of Bath stone. The nineteenth-century decoration in the hallway features marbleised walls and a ceiling with blue sky and clouds.

The house was sold to the Wise-Gubbins family, and in time became the home of the five Gubbins sisters – all of whom were deaf. There is a unique collection of Victorian watercolours by Beatrice Gubbins, an indefatigable traveller. The Gubbins line had no heirs and the house passed to their relatives, the Russell family, who are the present owners of the house. Period furniture includes Irish Georgian pieces, Adam fireplaces and magnificent gilt mirrors.

Riverstown House

Glanmire, Cork

When the Italian stuccodores Paolo and Filippo Lafrancini came to Ireland in 1734, their first and most important early work was for Jemmett Browne, later Bishop of Cork. In the 1730s Dr Browne enlarged and remodelled the original 1602 Riverstown House. The Lafrancinis adorned the ceiling of the dining room with allegorical figures representing 'Time rescuing Truth from the Assaults of Discord and Envy', and also its walls with classical figures and exuberant Rococo flowers and foliage.

The house remained in the Browne family until the present century, but by the 1950s the house was empty and decaying. It was bought in 1965 by the present owners Mr and Mrs John Dooley, and sympathetically restored with the help of the Georgian Society.

Glin Castle

Glin, Co Limerick

The village of Glin is adjacent to the seat of the 29th Knight of Glin, a scion of the Fitzgerald clan, whose family has held it in succession for 700 years. During the Desmond rebellion of 1641, the old castle was beseiged by Sir George Carew and surrendered after a fierce hand-to-hand fight. The then Knight survived, only to fall at Kinsale a year later (the ruined keep is near the stream).

The present Gothic façade of Glin Castle (1789-1812), with its crenellations and gleaming white walls, gives the building the unworldly quality that fascinated the Georgians involved in the Gothic revival. The tranquil parkland setting, gingerbread Gothic gatelodges and beautiful location on the Estuary of the Shannon add to the overall effect.

Inside the present Knight of Glin, Desmond Fitzgerald, has added, over the past two decades, to the Castle's great collection of Irish furniture, making it one of the best there is. The hall is illuminated by a Venetian window overlooking a formally designed garden.

Overleaf: King John's Castle, Limerick, Co Limerick.

King John's Castle

Limerick, Co Limerick

Standing beside the river Shannon, this castle is one of the most impressively sited Norman castles in Ireland. Built between *c*.1200 and 1207 for King John, brother of Richard the Lionheart, it was the centre of Norman authority in the area. The Castle's position enabled it to defend the river frontier between the Gaelic west and the Norman Leinster and Munster. Much of the castle has been preserved; its quadrilateral form, with curtain walls and drum towers have survived. The west side stands on the river, where there are unspoilt views from the opposite bank. On the north side, is the original gateway with D-shaped towers.

Ormonde Castle

Carrick-on-Suir, Co Tipperary

Ormonde Castle (also known as Carrick-on-Suir Castle) dates from the fifteenth century. In 1568 a manor house was added by the 10th Earl of Ormonde, who had spent many years at the English Court (his cousin was Elizabeth I). Elizabeth was even said to have borne him a child when she was twenty years old, a story which still persists today.

Noted for its plasterwork, the long gallery was once hung with tapestries. The elaborately worked ceiling collapsed over the years, though fortunately enough of it remained to allow a full restoration to take place. Firing holes protecting the arched entrance-way are the only indication of defence in this serene, domesticated dwelling.

Cahir Castle

Cahir, Co Tipperary

Cahir Castle is one of Ireland's largest and best-preserved castles situated on a rocky island on the river Suir. It was built in the fifteenth century by successive members of the Bulter family, Lords of Cahir, on the site of a thirteenth-century Norman fortress, and restored in 1840 and 1964. It comprises an elaborate curtain wall between

Overleaf: Cahir Castle, Cahir, Co Tipperary.
Following page: Ormonde Castle, Co Tipperary.

round and square towers, enclosing a tall keep, in the restored rooms of which is a collection of early oak furniture and a working portcullis.

Lismore Castle

Lismore, Co Waterford

Lismore is poised dramatically on a scarp overlooking the river Blackwater. The castle which had become dilapidated, was virtually rebuilt for the sixth Duke of Devonshire (known as the 'Bachelor Duke'), between 1812 and 1858; he employed several different architects, including Joseph Paxton. There is a fine yew walk, said to be eight hundred years old.

Desmond Castle

Kinsale, Co Cork

Built as a custom house by the Earl of Desmond *c.*1500, Desmond Castle has an interesting history. It was occupied by the Spanish in 1601 and later used as a prison for captured sailors during the American War of Independence. It is known locally as the 'French Prison' after a tragic fire in which 54 prisoners, mainly French seamen, died in 1747.

Dromoland Castle

Newmarket-on-Fergus, Co Clare

The O'Briens of Dromoland descend from the great warrior, Brian Boru, king of Ireland who died in 1014. The present Dromoland Castle was built in about 1826 by Edward O'Brien, fourth Baronet, to the designs of the Pain brothers. It is set in elaborate formal gardens designed by John Aheron.

Adare Manor

Adare, Co Limerick

Adare Manor was built in the Tudor-Revival style by the second and third Earls of Dunraven between 1832 and 1862. Several architects were involved in its design, including the patrons themselves. The Great Gallery is one of the longest in Ireland, and is 132 feet in length, with a timbered roof and stained glass windows.

Derrynane House

Co Kerry

Derrynane House, which dates back to *c.*1702, is the ancestral home of Daniel O'Connell (1775-1847), lawyer, politician and statesman. O'Connell, known as 'the Liberator', was the first Roman Catholic to take his seat as a Member of Parliament at Westminster: his election was the catalyst for the Roman Catholic Relief Act of 1829. He is featured as one of the key historical figures in James Joyce's *Portrait of the Artist as a Young Man*, and the widest avenue in Dublin, Sackville Street, was renamed in his honour.

Derrynane House still contains some of O'Connell's personal possessions, and is situated on 120 hectares of parkland on the Kerry coast.

Left: Derrynane House, Co Kerry.

CONNACHT

Rockfleet Castle

Newport, Co Mayo

This relatively small tower-house was the principle residence of the great Pirate Queen, Grace O'Malley, whose powers were undisputed in the sixteenth century.

Granuaile, as she was known in Irish, was married at the age of fifteen to Donal O'Flaherty, heir apparent to the O'Flaherty kingdom of Connemara. However, his quarrels and disputes with his neighbours brought war and famine upon his dependents. It was not long before Grace was to emerge as leader of her husband's clan. Trading in hides, tallow, and wool exporting as far afield as Spain and Portugal, her business was supplemented with piracy at sea.

Donal O'Flaherty was killed in a property dispute, so Grace later married Sir Richard Burke, the owner of Rockfleet Castle, and established her fleet here in 1566.

The castle is a fine fifteenth- or sixteenth-century tower situated beside an inlet of Clew Bay. It has four stories and a corner turret, as well as a fireplace on the top floor. It was said to be besieged by an expedition in 1574 when the Sheriff of Galway hoped to capture it, but the invasion was driven off by Grace O'Malley and her band.

After Sir Richard Burke's death in 1583, Grace continued living in the castle with 'all her own followers and one thousand head of cows and mares'.

Left: Rockfleet Castle, Newport, Co Mayo.
Overleaf: Parke's Castle, Fivemile Bourne, Co Leitrim.

Parke's Castle

Fivemile Bourne, Co Leitrim

A restored Plantation manor-house situated on the shores of Lough Gill, it was built *c.*1620 by Captain Robert Parke who received lands confiscated from Sir Brian O'Rourke, subsequently indicted and hanged at Tyburn, London, in 1591 for sheltering Francisco de Cueller, an officer of the shipwrecked Armada in 1588. The castle incorporated the bawn wall of the O'Rourke Tower House, the foundations of which were revealed in recent excavations.

The Castle has been restored using Irish oak and traditional local craftmanship. It is a fine example of a fortified manor house, retaining its outer defensive features as well as its gatehouse and hall. Nearby on the Lough Gill lakeshore is an example of a sweathouse, a kind of medieval Irish sauna.

Lynch's Castle

Galway, Co Galway

Lynch's Castle is the only complete secular mediaeval building still standing in Galway today. It was heavily renovated in 1966 and converted into a bank, though some original features remain. The gargoyles can still be seen, as well as the coat of arms of King Henry VII, the Lynch family, and the Fitzgeralds of Kildare.

In 1493, James Lynch Fitzstephen, the Mayor of Galway, invited the son of a Spanish trader to stay in Galway. His son who was in love with a Galway woman, became jealous of the Spaniard and the lady's partiality to his father's guest. He stabbed the Spaniard, and confessed to his father. Despite the efforts of the Galway citizens, Fitzstephen arrested and tried his son. No executioner could be found to hang him, so Fitzstephen hanged his own son from an upstairs window in his house. The event is marked by the 'Lynch Stone' which commemorates unbending justice.

Athenry Castle

Athenry, Co Galway

Athenry is one of the most notable mediaeval walled towns surviving in Ireland, owing its foundation to Meiler de Bermingham who built his Castle there *c*.1250. It has a rectangular keep with outworks and the great three-storey tower, surrounded by defensive walls, is entered at first-floor level through an unusual decorated doorway.

Portumna Castle

Portumna, Co Galway

The impressive castle at Portumna was the seat of the Clanricarde Burkes, for so long the most important landowners in Co Galway. It was completed *c*.1617 by Richard Burke, 4th Earl of Clanricarde, but was accidentally destroyed by fire in 1826.

The castle is a large, symmetrical, three-storey building, rectangular in shape, with square projecting corner towers. It was one of the first buildings in Ireland with Renaissance features, and is also noted for the Jacobean-type gables on its roof. The castle is located overlooking Lough Derg and also Portumna Forest Park, which was once part of the demesne.

Aughnanure Castle

Oughterard, Co Galway

Built by the O'Flahertys around 1500, Aughnanure Castle lies in picturesque surroundings close to the shores of Lough Corrib. Standing on what is virtually a rocky island, this fine castle is a particularly well-preserved example of an Irish tower-house. It has six stories and is unusual in having two bawns. The inner one is well preserved along the riverside and has a rounded turret with a fine corbelled roof. The outer bawn also has a turret at the south-western corner, and encloses the sixteenth-century banqueting hall (of which some parts remain). On the the window of the banqueting hall there are some vine-scrolls and other motifs.

Lough Cutra Castle

Gort, Co Galway

Lough Cutra Castle is a handsome Regency residence designed by John Nash and built by the Pain brothers in 1816 for the Viscount Gort. It is beautifully situated on the lake shore, and having stood empty for forty years was restored in the early

1970s when the Victorian additions were removed.

Moore Hall

Cong, Co Mayo

The ruin of Moore Hall, the Georgian home of a celebrated Mayo family, is situated on a promontory overlooking Lough Carra. The best-known members of the family are John (1763-99), who was appointed president of the 'Provisional Republic of Connacht' during the French invasion in 1798; George Henry (1811-70), MP for Mayo and one of the leaders of the Tenant-Right Movement, and George (1852-1933), a novelist.

George Moore played a prominent role in the Irish Literary Renaissance and helped to found the Abbey Theatre. Considered one of greatest novelists, he described the area in his novel *The Lake* (1905). He died in London on 21 January 1933 and his cremated remains were buried on Castle Island in Lough Carra.

Strokestown Park

Strokestown, Co Roscommon

At the end of Ireland's widest main street – laid out by the 2nd Lord Hartland as the widest street in Europe – a Georgian Gothic arch leads to Strokestown Park, seat of the Mahon family (and later Hales-Pakenham-Mahon) from 1600 to 1979. The house was designed for Thomas Mahon in the 1730s by the German architect Richard Castle (or Cassels), and incorporates parts of an earlier tower-house. The central block is the residential part of the house. The north wing houses Ireland's last galleried kitchen (a gallery in the kitchen allowed the lady of the house to observe the culinary activity without ever having to feel a part of it), and the south wing is the elaborate vaulted stable – described by one observer as 'an equine cathedral'.

The house is now owned and managed by Westward Garage Ltd, the company which bought the house intact with its contents in 1979. Complementing the formal reception

Left: Aughnanure Castle, Oughterard, Co Galway.

rooms downstairs are the more intimate childrens' rooms upstairs (a bedroom, schoolroom, and fully equipped nursery). In the study a selection of documents dealing with the Irish potato famine of the 1840s are on view.

Clonalis House

Castlerea, Co Roscommon

Clonalis is the ancestral home of the O'Conors, Kings of Connaught and providers of the last High Kings of Ireland. The O'Conor inauguration stone, similar to the Stone of Scone which lies in Westminster Abbey, can be seen at Clonalis. The house (1880), the first mass concrete house to be built in Ireland, stands on lands which have belonged to the O'Conors for 1,500 years. Owen O'Conor was dispossessed for short periods in the seventeenth century, but the remarkable tenure survived despite wars and penal laws. A fascinating historic archive of over 100,000 documents is maintained at Clonalis, including a copy of the last Brehon Law judgement, handed down about 1580. The harp of Turlough O'Carolan (1670-1738), the blind Irish bard, is on display in the house (the O'Conors were his patrons). Other exhibits include costumes, uniforms and laces belonging to the family. The house is well furnished with Sheraton and Louis XV-style furniture. Family portraits spanning many centuries decorate the walls.

Frybrook House

Boyle, Co Roscommon

Built *c*.1750 for Henry Fry, who came to Boyle at the invitation of Lord Kingston, Frybrook House is an imposing Georgian-style three-storey house. Many of the rooms enjoy views of the Boyle River, which bordered part of the original six-acre property. The drawing room contains some of the finest examples of Georgian decorative plasterwork in existence. There is an oculus in the centre of the top storey, above a Venetian window. The house has no basement, which is unusual for a house of its size and period.

Lissadell House

Drumcliffe, Co Sligo

The bow windows of Lissadell House look across Sligo Bay. WB Yeats recalled them in his poem to the Gore-Booth sisters Eva and Constance: 'The light of evening, Lissadell. Great windows, open to the south.'

The Gore-Booths have lived at Drumcliffe for centuries and the present house, built near a previous castle and manor, was designed by the English architect, Francis Goodwin for Sir Robert Gore-Booth in the 1830s, and is still their home. The house is built from cut grey limestone blocks, quarried locally at Ballysodare in Co Sligo. Each block was delicately chiselled, and is framed by a half inch plain band. The house, considered rather austere, resembles Goodwin's work at Macclesfield Town Hall, in Cheshire (1826).

Lissadell holds the legacy of generations of colourful Gore-Booths, including the travel diaries of Sir Robert who mortgaged the estate to help the poor during the famine. His son Sir Henry was an explorer of note, remembered for having sailed to the rescue of the Arctic explorer Leigh Smith. Eva Gore-Booth was a poetess. Her sister Constance Markievicz took part in the Easter Rising in 1916. In 1918 Constance became the first woman to gain a seat in the Westminster Parliament. Both sisters were celebrated in Yeats' poem *In Memory of Eva Gore-Booth and Con Markievicz.*

The dining-room is unique, having both portraits of the family and overlifed-size figures of the butler, forester and gamekeeper painted on the pilasters by Count Casimir Markievicz (husband of Constance Gore-Booth). At the core of the house is a dramatic two-storey hallway lined with Doric columns leading to a double staircase of Kilkenny marble.

Kylemore Abbey

Letterfrack, Co Galway

Kylemore Abbey, with its myriad battlements and turrets, is dramatically situated at the foot of a hill overlooking Kylemore lough in the wilds of Connemara. The mullioned windows and oriel create an impression of fairytale beauty, resulting in this being the most photographed and admired building in the West of Ireland

It was built in the 1860s by James F Fuller and Usher Roberts for Mitchell Henry, MP and rich Liverpool merchant. He and his bride, Margaret Vaughan, whilst on their honeymoon, had been charmed by Connemara and the picturesque location of Kylemore Lodge, a shooting lodge which stood on the spot now occupied by the Abbey. Mitchell Henry bought this property and the nine acres of mountain bog and lakes in order to build their dream house. It was eleborate in its design, which included thirty-three bedrooms, a ballroom with a sprung floor and a Turkish bath.

The Henrys had nine children but when Margaret died, after contracting Nile Fever in Egypt, Henry returned to England and sold Kylemore. In 1920, Kylemore was acquired by Benedictine nuns who were seeking to establish an Abbey and school in Ireland.

Ashford Castle

Cong, Co Galway

Ashford Castle stands at the head of Lough Corrib. Benjamin Guinness, the Dublin brewer, bought the castle in 1855 and created a French *chateau* beside the existing house His son, Sir Arthur Guinness, first Lord Ardilaun, added on the castle and the Georgian shooting box in 1870 – employing JF Fuller and George Ashlin to design these additions.

He and his wife employed three hundred people to beautify the demesne, planting nearly one million trees and flowering scrubs. By 1915 one million pounds had been spent on the property – a considerable amount for that time.

Kylemore Abbey, Letterfrack, Co Galway.

Picture Credits

Irish Tourist Board: 12, 15, 20, 30, 90, 92, 112, 114, 151

Northern Irish Tourist Board: 6, 9, 16, 19, 23, 24, 35, 37, 38, 40, 42, 43, 44, 47, 50, 52, 54, 56, 58, 60, 62, 65, 70, 73.

Heritage Images: 67, 75, 80, 84, 96, 98, 102, 104, 116, 118, 122, 126, 130, 134, 136, 138, 140, 142, 146.

Belfast City Council 77

Further Reading

C E B BRETT (1967): *Buildings of Belfast 1700-1914* (London: Weidenfeld & Nicolson)

_____ (1996): *Buildings of County Antrim* (with photographs by MICHAEL O'CONNELL) (Belfast: Ulster Architectural Heritage Society and the Ulster Foundation)

_____ (1999) *Buildings of County Armagh* (with photographs by MICHAEL O'CONNELL) (Belfast: Ulster Architectural Heritage Society)

_____ (2002): *Buildings of North County Down* (with photographs by ANTHONY C.W. MERRICK) (Belfast: Ulster Architectural Heritage Society)

MARK BENCE-JONES (1988): *Irish Homes and Gardens from the Archives of County Life* (London: Aurum Press Ltd)

CHRISTINE CASEY and ALISTAIR ROWAN (1993): *North Leinster* in *The Buildings of Ireland* series (London: Penguin Group)

MAURICE CRAIG (1982): *The Architecture of Ireland from earliest times to 1880* (London: B T Batsford Ltd, and Dublin: Eason & Son Ltd)

JAMES STEVENS CURL (1986): *The Londonderry Plantation 1609-1914: The History, Architecture, and Planning of the Estates of the City of London and its Livery Companies in Ulster* (Chichester: Phillimore & Co Ltd)

DESMOND GUINNESS (1979): *Georgian Dublin* (London: B T Batsford Ltd)

PAUL LARMOUR (1987): *Belfast: An Illustrated Architectural Guide* (Belfast: Friar's Bush Press)

JACQUELINE O'BRIEN AND DESMOND GUINNESS *Great Irish Houses and Castles* (Weidenfeld and Nicolson, London 1992)

ALISTAIR ROWAN (1979): *North West Ulster* in *The Buildings of Ireland* series (Harmondsworth: Penguin Books)

Readers are also referred to the substantial publications of the Ulster Architectural Heritage Society, many of which deal with individual districts and their buildings. The Irish Georgian Society is also responsible for several admirable publications which can be consulted with profit.